Very few countries among those that now apply nuclear energy for peaceful purposes possess the entire "fuel cycle" in which the nuclear material undergoes all the steps from mining and processing to use in power or research reactors, to final disposal or storage of spent fuel and reaction products. Still, at many points in this fuel cycle it is possible to divert nuclear material away from its intended use, employing it instead for the construction of nuclear weapons. And the number of states that have at least some nuclear material that would lend itself to use for explosive purposes—or some facility that would permit the transformation of nuclear material for such a purpose—is growing.

The International Atomic Energy Agency was set up to promote the peaceful uses of atomic energy. In recognition of the dual character of atomic energy, the Agency was at the same time charged with ensuring that the activities with which it is concerned will not be used to further any military purpose. To this end the Agency applies its safeguards.

This book discusses some aspects of these safeguards. Its thesis is that all Agency safeguards—whether applied pursuant to bilateral arrangements or to multilateral agreements such as the Treaty of Tlatelolco—are as much measures to prevent or deter the proliferation of nuclear weapons as are the safeguards applied pursuant to the Treaty on the Non-Proliferation of Nuclear Weapons (NPT). Conversely, the purpose of the safeguards agreements concluded in connection with the NPT is basically the same as that of any other safeguards agreements to which the Agency is a party, although there may be differences in application. While, therefore, the book deals with Agency safeguards in general, it is equally relevant to any study of NPT safeguards.

The book is not intended as a comprehensive description of Agency safeguards. It does give an overview of the safeguards, something of their history, their applications to date, and suggestions for their further development. It also stresses some of the problems facing the Agency in the applica-

Safeguards Against
Nuclear Proliferation

SIPRI

Stockholm International Peace Research Institute

SIPRI is an independent institute for research into problems of peace and conflict, with particular attention to the problems of disarmament and arms regulation. It was established in 1966 to commemorate Sweden's 150 years of unbroken peace.

The financing is provided by the Swedish Parliament. The staff, the Governing Board and the Scientific Council are international. As a consultative body, the Scientific Council is not responsible for the views expressed in the publications of the Institute.

Governing board

SIPRI

Stockholm International Peace Research Institute

Sveavägen 166, S-113 46 Stockholm, Sweden
Cable: Peaceresearch, Stockholm Telephone: 08-15 09 40

Safeguards Against Nuclear Proliferation

A SIPRI MONOGRAPH

Stockholm International Peace Research Institute

The MIT Press
Cambridge, Massachusetts and
London, England

Almqvist & Wiksell
International
Stockholm, Sweden

Printed in Sweden by
Göteborgs Offsettryckeri AB
Stockholm 1975

PREFACE

Article VIII.3 of the Treaty on the Non-Proliferation of Nuclear Weapons (NPT) states that "Five years after the entry into force of this Treaty, a conference of Parties to the Treaty shall be held in Geneva, Switzerland, in order to review the operation of this Treaty with a view to assuring that the purpose of the Preamble and the provisions of the Treaty are being realized". This Review Conference will take place in May 1975.

The economic and technical restraints on the production of nuclear weapons, once severe, have steadily decreased. Through peaceful nuclear programmes, a number of states have now accumulated the technical expertise and knowledge and the fissile material necessary to produce nuclear weapons. As time passes this number will increase. Whether or not these states will take up their nuclear weapon option in the future will depend mainly on political considerations. For many states the main political barrier to proliferation is the NPT. And the future success of the NPT will depend to a large extent on the outcome of the 1975 Review Conference. Because this conference will be a crucial event in the field of arms control and disarmament, SIPRI has prepared a number of books on nuclear proliferation issues. The first, *Nuclear Proliferation Problems*, was published in March 1974. Another, *The Nuclear Age,* was published in March 1975.

Of central importance to the NPT is the question of nuclear safeguards. Article III of the Treaty establishes the framework within which international safeguards, specifically those of the International Atomic Energy Agency (IAEA), are to operate. Under the Treaty, the IAEA is given the special responsibility of providing safeguards for ensuring that non-nuclear-weapon countries do not engage in the manufacture of nuclear weapons or other nuclear explosive devices. All non-nuclear-weapon states party to the NPT are required to conclude an agreement with the IAEA for the application of safeguards on all nuclear materials used in their peaceful nuclear activities.

The purpose of this book is to review the operation of IAEA safeguards, both those that are applied under the NPT and those which countries have accepted under other agreements to date, and to highlight and discuss some of the problems associated with the application of safeguards.

The book was written by Mr Benjamin Sanders while visiting SIPRI in the autumn of 1974. Mr Sanders is an official of the International Atomic Energy Agency, but the opinions expressed in this paper should be considered his own and do not necessarily reflect the official views of the agency.

January 1975

Frank Barnaby
Director

CONTENTS

1. The background

Square-bracketed references, thus [1], refer to the list of references following the chapter.

I. *Introduction*

Nuclear energy may be a blessing. It can be used to generate electricity; it can serve as a research tool; it can be employed in medicine, in agriculture and in industry, for such various purposes as fighting cancer, improving the yield of cereal plants, combatting insect pests and controlling the quality of machinery. It can also be used in the most devastating weapon ever devised.

This is due to the dual nature of the principal elements involved in the nuclear process. Uranium—in essence a "stable" element—contains, for every one thousand atoms of the isotope 238, about seven atoms of uranium 235, which is "unstable" and gives off radiation, that is, it emits various kinds of particles, including neutrons. Under the right conditions, some of these neutrons will be absorbed by other uranium 235 atoms, resulting in the disintegration or "fission" of the atom. This fission process creates large amounts of energy, including heat that can be used to generate electrical power. Other neutrons may be "captured" by atoms of uranium 238, producing a new element, plutonium 239. Plutonium 239 in turn, once it is separated from the various fission products and from the uranium in which it has been produced, lends itself easily to the fission process and can be used as a source of energy, either by itself or when mixed with uranium. It is also the basic material for the atomic "fission" bomb. It is possible, by means of the so-called isotope enrichment process, to increase the proportion of uranium 235 in uranium to make it a more efficient fuel; 2 to 3 per cent enriched uranium is used in many power reactors; other types of reactors use highly enriched uranium. On the other hand, highly enriched uranium can be used both in "fission" bombs and in "fusion", or hydrogen, weapons. It is a matter of choice.

This choice may be exercised at several junctures in the nuclear fuel cycle. Natural uranium is mined, concentrated, refined and converted, and either first enriched, or immediately prepared for fabrication into reactor fuel. Enriched uranium can also be fabricated into reactor fuel or, if its enrichment is high enough, into a weapon. The natural or enriched uranium which is used as fuel is "burned" or irradiated in the reactor; when it comes out it contains fission products, plutonium and some unburned uranium. These elements are separated out in the so-called reprocessing plant. And here, again, a choice exists: should the resulting plutonium be used as fuel in a reactor, or for an explosive purpose? These are just two examples of points in the nuclear fuel cycle where such a choice can be made.

Very few countries among those that now apply nuclear energy for peaceful purposes possess the entire "fuel cycle" in which the nuclear material undergoes all the steps described here, but the number of states that have at least some nuclear material that would lend itself to use for explosive purposes—or some facility that would permit the transformation of nuclear material for such a purpose—is growing.

The International Atomic Energy Agency was set up to promote the peaceful

1

uses of atomic energy. In recognition of the dual character of atomic energy, it was at the same time charged with ensuring that the activities with which it is concerned will not be used to further any military purpose. To this end the Agency applies its safeguards.

This paper discusses some aspects of these safeguards. Its principal thesis is that all Agency safeguards—whether applied pursuant to bilateral arrangements or to multilateral agreements such as the Treaty of Tlatelolco——are as much measures to prevent or deter the proliferation of nuclear weapons as are the safeguards applied pursuant to the Treaty on the Non-Proliferation of Nuclear Weapons (NPT). Conversely, the purpose of the safeguards agreements concluded in connection with the NPT is basically the same as that of any other safeguards agreements to which the Agency is a party, although there may be differences in the application. While, therefore, the paper deals with Agency safeguards in general, it is equally relevant to NPT safeguards.

This paper is not intended as a comprehensive description of Agency safeguards. It merely highlights some aspects which the author considers to be particularly relevant at the present moment. It also stresses some of the problems facing the Agency in the application of safeguards, or confronting the states involved; both those which have accepted Agency safeguards or consider doing so and those whose policy it is to require the application of safeguards in respect of certain items they export——nuclear fuel, atomic facilities or special pieces of equipment.

II. *History*

For as long as there has been international exchange of information on atomic technology and one state has provided another with nuclear material and equipment there have been demands for some kind of assurance that such supplies would be used as agreed. The most important and obvious aspect of this assurance is contained in the concept of international nuclear safeguards.

This concept has been under discussion almost from the moment that it became obvious that the secrets of nuclear technology and the materials required could not remain the monopoly of a single nation. Indeed, already in November 1945 the term "safeguards" was used in the "Three Nation Agreed Declaration" on international atomic energy policy by the president of the United States and the prime ministers of Canada and the United Kingdom [1]. The resolution of the United Nations General Assembly, which established the United Nations Atomic Energy Commission (UNAEC), incorporated part of the text of this declaration, *inter alia* using the phrase "For effective safeguards by way of inspection and other means..." [2]. It is not the intention here to go into historical detail. It is nevertheless essential to realize that from the beginning of the atomic era, safeguards designed to ensure that nuclear activities would not further military purposes have played a part in international political thought [3].[1]

[1] As soon as it became apparent, in early 1939, that it should be possible to cause a fission chain reaction in uranium, scientists involved attempted to keep this discovery from spreading by self-imposed restrictions on exchanges of information about their work. See, for example, reference [3].

The first full-fledged proposal for a system of safeguards was contained in the so-called Acheson/Lilienthal Report. This was prepared jointly by a committee headed by the then assistant secretary of state of the USA and a board of consultants headed by the chairman of the Tennessee Valley Authority. It was intended as the basis for the US attitude to be taken in the UNAEC. Among its main conclusions, the report stated that safeguards could be effective only if combined with international control. The study became the basis for the proposal presented by the US representative, Mr Bernard Baruch, later briefly called the "Baruch Plan". This foresaw the creation of an international atomic development authority, under the aegis of the United Nations, which would have managerial control or ownership of all potentially dangerous atomic energy activities, and be in effect an international monopoly in the field of nuclear development. The general features of this plan have been adequately publicized [4].

It is important for the purpose of the present discussion to emphasize that both the Acheson/Lilienthal Report and the Baruch Plan use the concept of "safeguards" as consisting of more than mere verification ("inspection and other means") and as necessarily requiring adequate physical control. Both documents, as well as the above mentioned UN resolution, reflected the conviction that safeguards are needed to prevent the proliferation of the military use of atomic energy. Although these documents contain an element of disarmament——the UN resolution speaks of the "elimination from national armaments of atomic weapons"——such international safeguards were obviously not seen primarily as a disarmament measure but were in the first place intended as an assurance against nuclear armament by those states which did not yet have the capability of manufacturing atomic weapons. Thus, long before the concept of "proliferation" was formulated, non-proliferation was thought of as a corollary of the inevitable, if obviously not always desirable, spread of nuclear knowledge and capability. In other words the main purpose was "peaceful promotion without military proliferation".

The Baruch Plan and a number of counterproposals were the subject of long and heated debate, first in the UNAEC and subsequently in the Security Council and in the General Assembly of the United Nations. In 1949 the USSR detonated its first nuclear device and in 1952 the United Kingdom did the same. Meanwhile the USA had amassed a considerable stockpile of nuclear material for military purposes. Obviously, the grandiose scheme of establishing an international authority that would control all nuclear materials was no longer viable. Thus died the first attempt at non-proliferation through international ownership and control. In further attempts the disarmament aspect would be lacking but the non-proliferation idea would live on, particularly in US thinking. It was given new impetus in the proposals made by President Eisenhower to the United Nations General Assembly in December 1953. These proposals, the "Atoms for Peace Plan", were based on the idea that the peaceful uses of atomic energy could be furthered by the transfer of nuclear material from military to civilian uses [5]. An international atomic energy agency would be created through which all international cooperation in nuclear matters would be channelled. This agency would have at its disposal stocks of nuclear material to be allocated to peaceful pursuits. This "pool" of nuclear material would absorb quantities hitherto earmarked for military purposes and thus form a measure of arms reduction. The plan did not mention international safeguards, but the first sketches for the Statute of the International Agency foreseen in it already contained the Agency's right to carry out safeguards and to verify the material allocated to any state. Thus, the non-proliferation element came back into the picture, although in nowhere near as sweeping a manner as foreseen in the Baruch Plan. Whereas this plan was to have created an atomic world monopoly, at the time of President Eisenhower's Atoms for Peace Plan it must have been obvious to its sponsors that a number of states, other than those that had detonated explosive devices, had already ventured into atomic development. It was to be expected that even if the International Atomic Energy Agency would become the main supplier of nuclear materials and the main promotor of atomic development, and in so doing would extend its safeguards to a large proportion of the world's peaceful nuclear activities, some such activities might already have escaped the safeguards net. And even then, the safeguards would lack the elements of control and monopolistic ownership of the Baruch Plan.

After a series of negotiations that lasted almost two years, the Statute of the International Atomic Energy Agency was opened for signature on 20 October 1956. Its safeguards provisions —which had formed a particularly sensitive part of the negotiations and which were the result of compromises reached after long and extremely complicated deliberation are described throughout the text. The basic provision is contained in Article II, which requires the Agency to "ensure, so far as it is able, that assistance provided by it or at its request or under its supervision or control is not used in such a way as to further any military purpose". Article III A.5 authorizes the Agency to establish and administer safeguards in three categories of cases: (a) in connection with the assistance provided by the Agency or at its request, under its supervision or control: (b) at the request of the parties to any bilateral or multilateral arrangement; and (c) at the request of a state, to any nuclear activity of that state. Article XI F.4 provides that any project of the Agency for research on or development or practical application of atomic energy must include undertakings by the states involved that the assistance provided shall not be used in such a way as to further any military purpose and that the project shall be subject to safeguards.

The Statute does not contain any obligation for a state to submit to Agency safeguards, except where it is a beneficiary of an Agency project. In the other two categories of cases listed in Article III, the reason for accepting safeguards may be either the fact that the state concerned is a party to a legal instrument obliging it to accept such safeguards or has other reasons for doing so — most usually because it is the recipient of nuclear material or equipment and the state supplying this has made it a condition that Agency safeguards should be applied in connection with such items. The obligation to submit to safeguards may be contained in a bilateral agreement for the provision of nuclear material or installations, of which many have been concluded by the United States, the United Kingdom and Canada, which provides for the transfer to the IAEA of the safeguards function. It may also follow from a multilateral agreement such as the Treaty for the Prohibition of Nuclear Weapons in Latin America (the Treaty of Tlatelolco of 1967) or the Non-Proliferation Treaty. Although the IAEA Statute enables the Agency to accept safeguards responsibility in these various cases, this is not in itself sufficient. The Agency can only carry out safeguards on the basis of an agreement with the state or states concerned. The various types of safeguards agreements to which the Agency is a party are referred to elswhere in this report.

Article XII of the Statute lists the rights and responsibilities which the Agency has in respect of safeguards, to the extent that these are relevant to the project or arrangement in question: to examine the design of facilities; to require the maintenance of records and to have access to them; to require reports; to take measures to ensure that nuclear material under safeguards which is chemically reprocessed is not diverted to military purposes, and to require that such material remains under Agency safeguards or is temporarily deposited with the Agency. This Article also contains a general description of the rights of Agency inspectors, while providing that these may be accompanied by representatives of the state, and specifies what actions the Agency may take in case of non-compliance with the non-military-use undertaking. Article XIV, which refers, *inter alia*, to safeguards expenditure, classes these costs in general as "administrative expenses", except where such expenses are recoverable under safeguards agreements which provide accordingly.

The Statute merely provided the basis for the Agency's safeguards. It was never meant to be more than the framework of a safeguards system. The substance of such a system would have to be found in the agreements between the states concerned and the Agency. Naturally, in order to avoid drawing up specific safeguards procedures in each case, it was necessary to work out a set of procedures for uniform application, in connection with all safeguards agreements.

The first "draft regulations for the application of safeguards" were discussed by the Board in 1959. They formed the basis for the deliberations of a special working group whose efforts, early in 1961, resulted in the Agency's first safeguards document, "The Agency Safeguards System (1961)" [6]. The safeguards procedures contained in this document related only to reactors with less than 100 megawatts thermal output (MW [th]). The document foresaw that procedures covering other types of nuclear facilities would be developed as the probable need for them became evident. The new provisions were incorporated in a number of agreements but it was soon realized that their scope would have to be extended to reactors of over 100 MW(th). This extension was adopted in 1964 [6 a] and at the same time the Board appointed a new working group to review the safeguards system— a review already envisaged when the first system was drawn up.

At the time the first system was developed, the subject of safeguards had been highly controversial and the discussions often tense. Since then, the attitudes of a number of member states which had not previously been in favour of the Agency's safeguards activities had changed, and the talks on the review of the system took the form of serious consideration of the technical procedures necessary to obtain effective safeguards. In January 1965, after a total of 32 meetings. the working group (on which all members of the Board might be represented) presented its proposals to the Board. After consideration by the Ninth General Conference, the Board approved the revised system in September 1965 [7].

Immediately upon the adoption of the new system a beginning was made with its incorporation into the safeguards agreements concluded from that moment on. Most of the agreements previously concluded were, whenever they came up for extension, converted to take account of the new system. The system was extended in 1966 by additional provisions for reprocessing plants [8], and in 1968 by further provisions for safeguarding nuclear material in conversion and fabrication plants [9]. In 1967 the Board also discussed the possibility of extending the safeguards system to isotope separation (enrichment) facilities. This extension has not so far been prepared.[2]

The Agency's Safeguards System of 1965 (or the "INFCIRC/66/Rev.2 System" as it has become known) still forms the basis for the greater portion of the Agency's safeguards activities. In fact, at the time that the Non-Proliferation Treaty entered into force the Agency was party to safeguards agreements with 32 states. Most of these agreements were based on INFCIRC/66/Rev.2 and only a few on INFCIRC/26. As of 1 June 1974 there were 58 of these "old type" agreements in force.[3]

The Treaty on the Non-Proliferation of Nuclear Weapons was opened for signature on 1 July 1968. Immediately following this event, the director general of the International Atomic Energy Agency, in preparation for the Agency's role under the treaty, convened a group of consultants to advise him on the manner in which the Agency should apply safeguards in relation to a country's entire range of peaceful uses of nuclear energy, with a view to ensuring that such safeguards would be effective, economical and widely acceptable. Experts from Canada, Denmark, Hungary, the UK, the USA and the USSR met for various periods between October 1968 and the end of August 1969 [10]. Several expert panels were also called to advise on specific aspects of the Agency's future work, notably on the information requirements for the safeguards system and on systems analysis of nuclear fuel cycles.

The NPT entered into force on 5 March 1970; on 11 March the director general advised member states of the preparatory work done and under way in the Secretariat bearing on the manner in which the Agency could fulfill its responsibilities under the Treaty. In April the Board of Governors, following up on a proposal made by the British representative in February, adopted a resolution submitted by Italy, the United Kingdom and the United States which established a committee, on which any member state of the Agency could be represented if it so desired, to advise the Board as a matter of urgency on the Agency's responsibilities in relation to safeguards in connection with the NPT and in particular on the content of the agreements which would be required in connection with that treaty. All member states of the Agency were invited to communicate their views on the implications of the NPT to the Agency's activities in relation to safeguards, and the director general was asked to circulate these views and reports containing his own views. The committee, with Dr K. Waldheim as its chairman, first convened on 12

---

[2] The Agency's safeguards system to be applied in connection with the NPT, contained in IAEA document INFCIRC/153 "The Structure and Content of Agreements between the Agency and States required in Connection with the Treaty on the Non-Proliferation of Nuclear Weapons" does contain provisions that are applicable to uranium enrichment facilities. Specific reference to such facilities is made in paragraph 106(a), which includes isotope separation plants under the definition of "facility".

[3] Although the application of Agency safeguards in respect of 16 of them had been suspended, as the state had concluded an agreement in connection with the NPT; see page 22 below.

6

June 1970 and completed its work on 10 March 1971, after 82 meetings. Delegates from 48 member states participated. The committee's report was couched in the form of recommendations for the contents of safeguards agreements and, in fact, included a complete safeguards system designed to enable the Agency to apply safeguards under the new conditions created by the treaty. On 20 April 1971 the Board authorized the director general to use this material as the basis for negotiating agreements required by Article III of the NPT.[4] It has formed the substance of every safeguards agreement so far concluded pursuant to NPT.

References

1   Appendix No. 6 to "The International Control of Atomic Energy; Growth of a Policy", US Department of State, Publication No. 2702 (Washington, 1946).

2. Resolution adopted by the UN General Assembly during the first part of its First Session, 24 January 1964 (Church House, Westminster, London), p. 9.

3. Goldschmidt, B., *Les Rivalités atomiques 1939–1966*, (Paris, Fayard, 1967), p. 27.

4. "International Control of Atomic Energy Policy at the Crossroads", US Department of State, Publication No. 3161 (Washington, June 1948). See also "The Baruch Plan: US Diplomacy Enters the Nuclear Age", US Government Printing Office, Publication No. 81–431 (Washington, 1972), prepared for the Subcommittee on National Security Policy and Scientific Development of the US Congressional Committee on Foreign Affairs. The various proposals are described extensively in Szasz, Paul C. (see below, ref. no. 11); he quotes at length from the Acheson/Lilienthal Report (published as "Report on the International Control of Atomic Energy", Publication No. 2498 of the US Department of State (Washington, March 1946).

5. Häfele, W., "NPT Safeguards in Nuclear Proliferation Problems", in Jasani, B., ed., *Nuclear Proliferation Problems*, (Stockholm, Almqvist & Wiksell, Stockholm International Peace Research Institute; Cambridge, Mass. and London, the MIT Press), pp. 143–144.
    143–144.

6. International Atomic Energy Agency Document INFCIRC/26.
    (*a*)––, INFCIRC/26/Add. 1.

7. INFCIRC/66: "The Agency's Safeguards System (1965)".

8. INFCIRC/66/Rev.1.

9. INFCIRC/66/Rev.2.

10. GOV/INF/212, Annex.

[4] INFCIRC/153, also called "the Blue Book". A comparison between INFCIRC/66/Rev.2 and INFCIRC/153 is given in chapter 3. The two documents are reproduced as appendices.

2. Some basic issues

I. *The objective of safeguards*

Agency document INFCIRC/66/Rev. 2, which contains the Safeguards System of 1965, has the stated purpose of establishing a system of controls to permit the Agency to comply with its statutory obligation of ensuring that assistance provided by it or at its request or under its supervision or control is not used in such a way as to further any military purpose. The document does not set out the technical objectives of the safeguards system it contains, nor does it specify what conclusions are to be drawn from the verification activities, or what statements the Agency should seek to make. The only reference to such a statement is found in the so-called "Inspectors' Document", which states that after an inspection has been carried out, the Agency shall inform the state concerned of its results.[1]

The objective of safeguards applied pursuant to document INFCIRC/153 is the timely detection of diversion of significant quantities of nuclear material from peaceful nuclear activities to the manufacture of nuclear weapons or of other nuclear explosive devices or for purposes unknown, and deterrence of such diversion by the risk of early detection. The "Blue Book" further provides that the technical conclusion of the Agency's verification activities shall be a statement, in respect of each material balance area, of the amount of material unaccounted for over a specific period, giving the limits of accuracy of the amounts stated. Thus, NPT safeguards are directed at quantitative statements that leave room for reasonable judgement. The feed-back from the Agency to the state is one of the main features of the system and gives an additional justification for the flow of information from the state to the Agency.

Besides the statements on the technical conclusions derived from verification, the Agency is required, twice a year, to inform each government of the nuclear material inventory it has on its books for the state concerned. This permits a check on the completeness of the information flow. Further, at intervals to be specified in the Subsidiary Arrangements, the Agency should inform the state of the results of its inspections. In this way NPT safeguards assure a thorough exchange of information between safeguarder and safeguardee [1]. The Agency's Safeguards System of 1965 lacks any provision regarding the kinds of statements to be made after inspections. The only, indirect, guidance to its contents is in the Statute [2a]. This merely indicates that a statement by the Agency would consist of a declaration of whether or not there is compliance with the State's undertaking not to use "the assistance provided" (that is, the nuclear material concerned) in such a way as to further any

---

[1] GC(V)INF/39, Annex, paragraph 12. This document, which is in the form of a memorandum by the Director General, approved by the Board, gives rules for the designation of Agency inspectors, inspection notice, rights of access and privileges and immunities of Agency inspectors, in connection with the application of Agency safeguards. The NPT-type agreements themselves contain rules that are similar to and partly identical with those given in this document.

military purpose, which, if it is not qualified further, would imply an undifferentiated "yes-no" statement.

In practice, statements under the older system have so far consisted of the flat announcement that "the inspection has not revealed any departure from the terms of the agreement", although of course there have been minor deviations: delays in reporting, mistakes in record keeping, omission of notifications required by the agreement, and so on. None of these have been of a nature which would have warranted, in the view of the Agency's management, reporting the matter to the Board of Governors, and invoking the sanctions described in the Statute: a call on the state to "remedy forthwith" the non-compliance, a report to all the Agency's members, to the Security Council and to the General Assembly of the United Nations [2 a]. Moreover there has never been an occasion to take the measures anticipated should corrective action not be taken: curtailment or suspension of assistance and a call for the return of supplied material and equipment. The effectiveness and – in fact – the enforceability of such measures is open to some doubt, as is the potential impact on a delinquent government of the ultimate step foreseen in the Statute, suspending it from "the exercise of the privileges and rights of membership". The one really punitive aspect in this enumeration of steps might be the publicity that would result from a report to the United Nations. And it is in any case valid to question the likelihood of a state which has voluntarily accepted the application of safeguards consciously breaching its obligations, rather than having recourse to the termination clause contained in each safeguards agreement. In this respect the provision of the Safeguards System of 1965, that in the event of "any non-compliance . . . with a safeguards agreement" the statutory sanctions may be invoked is perhaps somewhat unrealistic. None but the most flagrant case of diversion would prompt the Agency to set in motion the ponderous machinery of statutory sanctions.

The NPT agreements, on the other hand, both contain easier ways to invoke sanctions and measures that enable the Agency to react not only once there has been an obvious breach of the agreement, but already at an earlier stage. They provide that the Board may decide, upon report of the director general, that an action by the state is essential and urgent to enable the Agency to verify that there has been no diversion; in such a case, the Board can call on the state to take the required action. This article [3 a] may be invoked, for instance, if the state should obstruct the application of safeguards, withhold required information or refuse access for the purpose of inspection to locations of safeguarded nuclear material. In addition, the agreements allow the Board to invoke the statutory sanctions also if it finds that the Agency is unable to verify that there has been no diversion. Accordingly, whereas previously the burden of proof would have been on the Agency to say that there has been "non-compliance", this provision [3 b] means that a lack of information may also result in sanctions. Presumably, the Board would not take such a step without calling on the state to remedy its actions. Moreover, the article in question enjoins the Board to "take account of the degree of assurance provided by the safeguards measures that have been applied" and to "afford the State every reasonable opportunity to furnish the Board with any necessary reassurance".

Neither provision has yet had to be called upon, but it is obvious that, before the

Agency caused the machinery of sanctions to be set in motion, the state would be given every possible opportunity to explain itself and to mend its ways. It is also apparent that, here again, the practical effect of such measures cannot be more than a public condemnation, and perhaps the termination of nuclear supplies by other states. How much impact this would have when a state is bent on diversion remains to be seen.

II. *Peaceful uses*

The purpose of Agency safeguards is given in Article II of the Statute: to "ensure ... that assistance provided by the Agency or at its request or under its supervision or control is not used in such a way as to further any military purpose". Article III A.5 authorizes the Agency to "establish and administer safeguards" to this end, both in respect of its own projects and of bilateral or multilateral arrangements or of the nuclear activities of a single state. (Incidentally, while the term "military purpose" is used several times in the main Statute article on Agency safeguards, Article XII, this prescribes that special fissionable material recovered through reprocessing shall be used only for "peaceful purposes", under continuing Agency safeguards.) The question is what these "military purposes" are, against which safeguards are applied or, conversely, what the peaceful purposes are which are the only ones for which nuclear materials safeguarded by the Agency may be used.

This question was raised after 18 May 1974, when India detonated a nuclear device. India declared that its underground explosion was a "peaceful nuclear experiment" and that it had no intention of developing nuclear weapons [4]. As far as is known, the material used in the experiment was produced in a research reactor constructed under the agreement between Canada and India which provided that "the reactor and any products resulting from its use (would) be employed for peaceful purposes only".[2] If the material used in the Indian explosion had been under IAEA safeguards — which it was not — would its use for a "peaceful nuclear experiment" have been a contravention of the safeguards agreement?

The Agency's Statute expressly requires an undertaking by the state or states aided by an Agency-assisted project, that the assistance shall not be used in such a way as to further any military purpose [2 b]. The Agency's Safeguards System of 1965 says that a "safeguards agreement" is any agreement" ... which contains an undertaking by one or more ... States not to use certain items in such a way as to further any military purpose and which gives the Agency the right to observe compliance with such undertaking" [5 a].

What undertaking? For the agreements concluded in connection with the NPT the answer is given in Article III.1 of the treaty. The basic undertaking of the Article is repeated in the "Blue Book", which further provides that the objective of safeguards is "the timely detection of diversion of significant quantities of nuclear

[2] Agreement on the Canada-India Colombo Plan Atomic Reactor Project, of 28 April 1956, Article III, covering the "Cirus" research reactor. Since this agreement was concluded, the government of Canada has made it clear that it considered this phrase also as prohibiting the use of the reactor and of materials produced in it for the purpose of developing a nuclear explosive device. On 1 October 1971 Prime Minister Trudeau recorded this interpretation in a letter to the Prime Minister of India, Mrs. Gandhi.

material from peaceful nuclear activities to the manufacture of nuclear weapons or of other explosive devices" [3 c]. "Or of other nuclear explosive devices"; the treaty knows no distinction between the purposes for which these devices should be manufactured; the underlying assumption is that the technology involved in the manufacture of any nuclear explosive device is indistinguishable from that involved in making a nuclear weapon [6 a, 8 a].[3] The distinction can only be in the mind of the firer" [7].

But must one read the phrase of the Statute ". . . not . . . to further any military purpose" as including any explosive nuclear device, also in the context of "INFCIRC/66/Rev. 2 Safeguards"? This conclusion has lately been expressed by some sponsors of the NPT. In March 1972 the member of the Board of Governors for the United States declared that the ability of the United States to provide source or special fissionable material, and other material, equipment or devices under all agreements for cooperation in the civil uses of atomic energy was predicated on the following understandings: first, that the guarantees with respect to the use of items subject to such agreements for cooperation with the United States precluded the use of such items for any nuclear explosive devices; and, secondly, that any safeguards agreements related to such bilateral agreements would continue to assure verification, *inter alia*, that the safeguarded material was not used for any nuclear explosive device.

In June 1972, the governor from the United Kingdom similarly stated that commitments regarding the use of items subject to cooperation agreements on the possible uses of nuclear energy to which the United Kingdom was party (and he stressed that this included those that had been entered into prior to the entry into force of the NPT) precluded their utilization for any type of nuclear explosive device. Safeguards agreements would, *inter alia*, continue to include verification that the safeguarded material was not being used for such a device. The United States reiterated its stand at the General Conference in September 1974, and on 3 October the US Representative wrote a letter along the same lines to the Director General. This is reproduced in Annex 1. Recently, also, in connection with the proposed supply of a nuclear power station to Argentina, Canada stated that it was its policy that such supplies would be used only for peaceful purposes and would in particular not be used for the development or manufacture of any nuclear explosive devices.

The interpretation that Agency safeguards applied pursuant to INFCIRC/66/Rev. 2 should also ensure that the items covered by them would not be used in the manufacture of any nuclear explosive device is not only relevant in connection with agreements governed by the Agency's pre-NPT safeguards system but also has a bearing on the execution of the NPT itself. Article III.2 of that treaty provides that parties undertake not to provide nuclear material or special equipment to any non-nuclear-weapons state for peaceful purposes "unless the source or special fissionable material shall be subject to the safeguards required by this Article". Obviously, such safeguards are intended, in the light of Articles I and III.1 of the

[3] In a paper by Dr S. von Welck, "Rechtsprobleme friedlicher Kernsprengungen unter besonderer Berücksichtigung des NV-Vertrags", delivered to the First International Meeting on Nuclear Law of "Nuclear Inter Jura 73", the approach laid down in the NPT is qualified as the "pessimistic solution". See reference [8 a].

treaty, to ensure against the manufacture and acquisition of any form of nuclear explosive. It has been accepted, at least by a number of supplier states, that safeguards pursuant to INFCIRC/66/Rev. 2 and NPT safeguards must serve the same purpose in this respect.

Anyway, if it is correct to see the NPT as merely one of a series of measures intended to prevent the proliferation of nuclear weapons, it follows that the steps which preceded the treaty were intended to have the same effect, and that all Agency safeguards are meant as anti-proliferation measures. The fact that "peaceful nuclear explosions" may not, at an earlier stage, have been expressly listed among prohibited activities must be ascribed rather to their then still more or less theoretical character than to any conscious wish to ignore them. On the contrary. The Acheson/Lilienthal Report of 1946 classed "the study of atomic explosives" among the "intrinsically dangerous activities", even though it realized that it might "yield by-products useful in peaceful activities". The report insisted that such studies should be under the exclusive purview of the proposed International Atomic Development Authority.

This is the first time that the Agency is faced with the question. Whatever its attitute in the past— and it is doubtful whether one can honestly say that this has been its conscious approach all along—there is now a clear trend to interpret safeguards "designed to ensure that special fissionable and other material . . . are not used in such a way as to further any military purpose" as including safeguards against the use of such material for any nuclear explosive device, whatever its intended use.[4] Incidentally, the use of safeguarded nuclear material for, to offer an example, the nuclear propulsion of naval vessels is also excluded in agreements concluded under INFCIRC/66/Rev. 2.

It is legitimate to ask what the Agency would do if it were confronted with a wish of a state party to the Treaty of Tlatelolco, with which it has a safeguards agreement, to manufacture an explosive device for peaceful purposes.[5] So far, all but one of the safeguards agreements between the Agency and states party to the Treaty of Tlatelolco are also concluded in connection with the NPT; the question could not properly be raised by a state party to such a dual purpose instrument. There is one NPT-type agreement concluded with a state that is a party only to the Treaty of Tlatelolco. But this also contains an undertaking identical to those

[4] Nevertheless, the Agency's Board of Governors as a body has never made a formal statement to this effect.

[5] To use the words of Dr von Welck [8 b]: In the Tlatelolco Treaty (Treaty for the Prohibition of Nuclear Weapons in Latin America, 14 February 1967, published in UN Treaty Series No. 9068)—which, in Article 18 makes provision for "Explosions for Peaceful Purposes", which contracting Parties are formally, but under certain restrictive conditions permitted to carry out—the "optimistic solution" is chosen. That is to say, a distinction is made between "nuclear weapons" and "nuclear devices for peaceful purposes"—this distinction being evidently based on the intention of the parties. An apparent attempt to make the optimistic or "declared intention" approach more objective, was made recently when a member of the Agency's Board of Governors suggested that only nuclear explosions carried out under international observation could be deemed to be peaceful. It is not entirely clear, however, how international observation would deprive the explosion of a nuclear device of its potential "test" character. Further, it could be applied only to explosions carried out by non-Parties to NPT on their own territory or that of other non-Parties. (Author's translation.)

accepted by states party to the NPT, namely to accept safeguards ". . . for the exclusive purpose of verifying that (source or special fissionable material in all its peaceful nuclear activities) is not diverted to nuclear weapons or other nuclear explosive devices". On the basis of the Treaty of Tlatelolco, however, another solution might be thought of, by which peaceful nuclear explosives would not be proscribed. In the thinking that prevails at present, it is by no means certain that the Agency could accept such a solution.[6]

III. *Standardization*

All safeguards agreements concluded in connection with the NPT are based on and incorporate the substance of INFCIRC/153. They are to a very large extent uniform, except for some specific provisions such as those regarding entry into force and the suspension of the application of Agency safeguards under other agreements. Agreements concluded pursuant to the Agency's Safeguards System of 1965 show perceptible variations. Document INFCIRC/66/Rev. 2 does not contain the "structure and content of agreements" as does INFCIRC/153. It gives principles and procedures for the application of safeguards, which must be further elaborated in the appropriate agreements. Its intention is to give guidance, to help states "to determine in advance the circumstances and manner in which the Agency would administer safeguards . . .and to enable the Board and the Director General to determine readily what provisions should be included in agreements relating to safeguards and how to interpret such provisions"[5 b]. These provisions will only become legally binding to the extent that they are incorporated in a safeguards agreement [5 c], and the extent to which they are incorporated depends on the given situation. The document itself is flexible in this respect. It merely enjoins the Agency not to assume safeguards responsibility unless "the principles of the safeguards and the procedures to be used" as contained in the relevant agreement are "essentially consistent" with those of INFCIRC/66/Rev. 2 [5 d]. This of course leaves room for deviation. In addition, the relevant agreement further elaborates the procedures, particularly in respect of notifications of transfers of nuclear material, the structure of the inventory of nuclear materials to be kept by the Agency and other very basic points which, in fact, determine the scope of the application of safeguards. Thus, INFCIRC/66/Rev. 2 cannot be considered in isolation from the various agreements based on it.

There are three main categories of such safeguards agreements: (1) those by which parties to a bilateral agreement for cooperation in the nuclear field transfer to the Agency the right and obligation to apply the safeguards foreseen in such agreements---the so-called "Safeguards Transfer Agreements"; (2) those by which states submit all or more often a defined part of their peaceful nuclear activities to Agency safeguards---the so-called "Unilateral Submission Agreements": and (3) those pertaining to assistance provided by the Agency---"Project Agreements". Safeguards transfer agreements are usually open-ended; they make it possible

---

[6] The Agency's approach has not yet been put to the test. Even among states that may be assumed to disagree with it, none has so far suggested using Agency safeguarded material for nuclear explosions.

for the safeguards to be extended to any item provided under the bilateral agreement. As a rule, unilateral submission agreements pertain to given facilities or specific supplies of nuclear material. The same is true of project agreements. The content of the agreements will naturally vary according to the subject. The procedures provided for in the various agreements concluded under INFCIRC/66/Rev.2 may vary one from the other, depending on the extent and the form in which provisions of the document are incorporated and elaborated in them. This is one of the reasons why the Agency's Board of Governors has been calling for greater standardization in the agreements concluded under the Safeguards System of 1965.

In practice, however, the *application* of safeguards within the category of INFCIRC/66/Rev. 2 agreements is less varied. Both for political and operational and technical reasons the Secretariat makes every attempt to apply uniform safeguards procedures so that, *mutatis mutandis*, each state receives the same treatment and different facilities are dealt with to the extent possible in a similar manner, so that discrimination is avoided as fas as possible. The subsidiary arrangements that are described elsewhere in this volume[7] are an important instrument in the standardization of application.

Standardization may not always be a virtue. If it is indiscriminately applied it may actually be counter-productive. In theory it might be easier to standardize application under the Agency's Safeguards System of 1965 than in respect of NPT safeguards. The latter system is designed to take advantage of the fact that all nuclear material in peaceful activities of the state is under safeguards. This makes it possible to stipulate that the main inspection effort should be concentrated at those stages in the nuclear fuel cycle where there is nuclear material in such a form as to lend itself most easily to the manufacture of nuclear explosives [3 d]. The Agency's Safeguards System of 1965, on the other hand, was designed in the first place to serve as the basis for the kind of agreement by which single facilities, or a limited number of them, are made subject to safeguards. It is primarily facility-oriented, and as a result each facility may bear the full weight of safeguards procedures. Applied in an undifferentiated manner, independently from the other nuclear activities of the state, such a standardized approach might be unduly burdensome. Standardization must not lead to indiscriminate uniformity.

Within the Secretariat the process of standardization is a complicated one which has to take account not only of technical but also legal, political and economic factors. This makes it necessary for many items of outgoing correspondence, notably concerning subsidiary arrangements, as well as internal papers, such as inspection instructions or verification procedures, to go through a process of careful consultation to ensure that besides the similarity of approach that must be achieved in all comparable situations, all relevant aspects involved in that approach are adequately dealt with. For this purpose, use is made of various means of internal coordination, such as standing interdisciplinary working groups or committees, and precisely prescribed channels of clearance. The policies worked out in this way and the precedents thus established are subsequently codified for further reference. It is one of the main preoccupations of safeguards management that such policies and

7 See "Subsidiary Arrangements", p. 25, *et seq.*

precedents are regularly brought to the attention of all those who have to apply them.

IV. *Pursuit*

In one respect Agency safeguards agreements outside the NPT system may vary considerably. This concerns the concept of the "pursuit" or "follow-up" of special fissionable material produced in or by the use of safeguarded nuclear material, facilities, equipment or such non-nuclear material as heavy water. This concept implies the principle that the supply of any nuclear item should *never* further any military purpose and thus that nuclear material produced by means of or with the help of such items should also come under safeguards, and that further generations of material issuing directly or indirectly from the produced material should also be covered. "Pursuit" may exist both in space and in time. Territorially, safeguards may be stipulated to follow material, wherever it is exported; conversely, neither a shift to another facility nor export is possible without safeguards. Time-wise, safeguards follow generation after generation of produced material. Both aspects of pursuit are implicit in the Agency's Safeguards System of 1965. The concept has formed a prime element in the non-proliferation approach contained in the Agency's safeguards system that preceded the NPT. In fact, already in the early years it was realized that if this principle of "derivation" or "contamination" [9 a] is closely adhered to, it would, through the use of safeguarded material and facilities in conjunction with unsafeguarded items, lead to a "proliferation of safeguards" from which eventually an international safeguards web could be spun through which little, if any, unsafeguarded material would be able to escape.

The concept was not always fully adhered to, however. The Safeguards System of 1965, referring to the provision of the Statute authorizing the Agency to require that reprocessed special fissionable material should remain under Agency safeguards, states that it is desirable that agreements should provide for the continuation of safeguards with respect to such material [5 e]. In other words, safeguards would continue without a time restriction. Many safeguards agreements contain an express provision to this effect.[8] In connection with others, the governments concerned have given indications that, on the expiration of the agreement, the question of continued safeguards on produced material would be considered. Some agreements, however, contain clauses limiting their initial duration while ignoring the question of continued safeguards on produced material. It follows that, unless their validity is extended, safeguards on nuclear material previously covered by the agreement will cease.[9]

[8] For example, the agreement between Switzerland, the USA and the Agency, of 28 February 1972. This "safeguards transfer agreement" is reproduced in Agency document INFCIRC/161.

[9] For example, the agreement between the Agency and Argentina for the application of safeguards to the Atucha Power Reactor of 3 October 1972. This "unilateral submission agreement" is reproduced in Agency document INFCIRC/168. A variation is found in the "safeguards transfer agreement" between Canada, India and the Agency, regarding the Rajasthan Atomic Power Station, which besides providing for an initial period of validity of five years, states that nuclear material produced by the use during the first five years of heavy water supplied by Canada, and all subsequent generations of nuclear material produced in or by the use of such nuclear material, shall be subject to Agency safeguards. Otherwise, however, safeguards apply only to nuclear material provided by Canada for, and nuclear material produced in, the power station. This agreement is reproduced in INFCIRC/211.

NPT type agreements provide that they shall remain in force as long as the state is party to the treaty. During that period, of course, safeguards pertain simply to all nuclear material in all peaceful nuclear activities in the country. The "geographical" pursuit of material is determined by Article III.2 of the treaty, which assumes that the state will see to it that it does not export relevant items, including nuclear material, without safeguards.

Recently, the Board of Governors decided in favour of a greater degree of standardization with respect to the duration and termination of agreements that will be concluded in future under the Agency's Safeguards System of 1965. It formally adopted the policy that such agreements should reflect the following two concepts: (a) that the agreement should remain in force as long as nuclear material, equipment, facilities or non-nuclear material supplied to the state, in connection with which safeguards are to be applied, are in actual use in the state, and (b) that the provisions for terminating the agreement should be such that the safeguards continue to apply in connection with any supplied material or items and to any special fissionable material produced, processed or used in or in connection with supplied material or items on the inventory of safeguarded items. Safeguards would cease only when they are no longer relevant in terms of the safeguards system. The point is of interest, not only in order to ensure the traditional non-proliferation character of the Agency's Safeguards System of 1965 but also to make that system suitable to serve as the "safeguards required by" Article III.2 of the NPT.

The Board's decision was not inflexible however. It says that the two concepts should "normally" be reflected in agreements, and adds the understanding that if the governments in question consider that there are exceptional reasons for departing from them, the matter should be brought to the Board for settlement. It would then be up to those governments to justify such departure. There may well be objection on the part of some governments, particularly those entering into a so-called "unilateral submission agreement", in which the supplier of the material or equipment concerned is not directly involved. The Board has recently confirmed that the two concepts are equally valid for this category of agreements as for any other concluded under the Safeguards System of 1965, including the tripartite safeguards transfer agreements. In so doing, it has met the wishes of supplier states, particularly those that are parties to the NPT, who may not make certain exports without the safeguards "required by this Article" and who wish to make sure that certain minimum criteria are met.[10] But also those not party to the treaty need to consider the restraints they wish to impose on the use of their supplies.

V. *Article III.2*

This is a crucial part of the treaty. Adequate safeguards arrangements not only require a state to undertake to use its nuclear material for certain purposes and to accept that its observance of that undertaking is supervised; they also require that nuclear material is not exported without safeguards being applied to it at its

[10] See also below, pp. 20–21.

destination,[11] and that material and equipment particularly suitable and fabricated to be used for nuclear purposes should only be sold abroad on condition that the nuclear activity for which they are intended will in turn be covered by safeguards.

As a rule the Agency's agreements under the Safeguards System of 1965 contain provisions regulating the export of nuclear material in this sense. But there has never before been general agreement among suppliers to make the export of nuclear material, important items of equipment for nuclear use, or non-nuclear materials of particular usefulness in nuclear activities conditional on safeguards at the receiving end. The case of the trade in heavy water illustrates the absence of such a general agreement in the past. The United States—a large supplier of this non-nuclear material, which is used in reactors capable of producing high grade plutonium—has always made safeguards a condition of supply. The same is true for several other states. But others have offered heavy water without requiring safeguards, at a higher price, dictated perhaps less by high production costs than by the producer's view that a higher price justifies a certain risk or, conversely, that freedom of action should be paid for. Clearly, commercial competition has often taken priority over political wisdom.[12]

The commercial argument was recognized during the negotiations on the NPT, and Article III.2 was one result. But, to be effective, it assumed a true measure of solidarity among supplier states. Some governments may not be able to accept political commitments that put their industry at a disadvantage *versus* the industries of other states, even for the sake of international security.[13]

The manner in which Article III.2 is implemented is a matter for exporting states party to the treaty. The Agency, not being a party, is involved insofar as it administers the safeguards which are required in the importing state. The exporters determine the requirements. But the article does not give complete guidance on the way it should be implemented. Therefore, representatives of a group of exporting states met soon after the Agency Safeguards Committee had completed its work, to consider procedures in relation to the exports of certain categories of equipment and material. Their purpose was to reach a common understanding on the way in which each state would interpret and implement its commitment under Article III.2, with a view to agreeing conditions for fair commercial competition with respect to this implementation.

One of the points at issue was the designation of the items of equipment and material which, in the language of the Article, were "especially designed or prepared for the processing, use or production of special fissionable material". The supply of such items should bring about Agency safeguards in respect of the nuclear

[11] The concept of "territorial pursuit".

[12] See Barnaby F., "Last chance for sanity", in *New Scientist*, 11 July 1974: ". . . since the nuclear economic stakes are now so huge . . . international nuclear dealings are carried out more and more between industrial firms on the basis of ordinary commercial rules and competition than of national interest" [p. 64].

[13] For example: In 1966 the government of the Federal Republic of Germany declared its readiness to include in all its contracts for the supply of nuclear materials and equipment to countries outside the area of the European Communities a clause requiring safeguards to be applied by the Agency, *provided other supplying countries were willing to impose the same condition*. Compare statement of the German delegate at the Tenth Regular Session of the Agency's General Conference GC(X)/OR.104, paragraph 117.

material produced, processed or used in the facility for which such items were supplied. A similar subject had arisen once before, during the discussion on the Agency's Safeguards System of 1965. A provision was included in this document that nuclear material should, *inter alia*, be subject to Agency safeguards if it is produced, processed or used in a "principal nuclear facility" which has been "supplied wholly or substantially under a project agreement". It was left up to the Board to determine what supplies would lead to the facility having to be considered as "substantially supplied"; no explicit rules were incorporated in the document. The Board, and the working group which drafted the system, spent some time on an attempt to define the type of supplies which should trigger the application of safeguards. They were unsuccessful, and it was left to the Board to determine in each separate case what supplies of non-nuclear material and equipment have a triggering effect in the case of project agreements. In other agreements concluded under the Safeguards System of 1965 it depends on the governments party to them what supplies are adequate to bring about the application of safeguards to the nuclear material in the facility concerned [9 b].

The group of suppliers deliberated for several years. In July 1974 they reached a common understanding on the procedures to be followed for the supply of nuclear materials as well as in connection with the supply of equipment and non-nuclear material. In August 1974, 10 states[14] informed the director general of the IAEA that for exports of source or special fissionable material, as described in Article XX of the Agency's Statute, to any non-nuclear-weapon states for peaceful purposes, they would require as a pre-condition of supply that such material should not be diverted to nuclear weapons or other nuclear explosive devices. They would satisfy themselves that safeguards to that end would be applied to the material in question, under an agreement with the IAEA and in accordance with its safeguards system. They also informed the Agency that when making such exports they would require assurances that the material would not be re-exported to a non-nuclear-weapon state not party to the NPT unless arrangements for Agency safeguards were made by the state receiving such re-export. For the purpose of these procedures, quantities of nuclear material below certain limits or to be used in non-nuclear activities would be disregarded. Secondly, the governments advised the director general that they had adopted procedures in relation to export of certain categories of equipment and material, as described in Article III.2 of the NPT. Having succeeded where previous attempts had failed, they had drawn up a list designating the categories of equipment and material, the export of which would "trigger" the application of safeguards to the nuclear material produced, processed or used in the facility for which these items were to be supplied.[15] This "trigger list" was meant as a minimum, with states concerned reserving the right to add items to it. As in the case of nuclear material, provisions were adopted in respect of re-transfer of items.

One question is answered neither by the "trigger list" nor by any of the existing safeguards documents: Does supply of know-how trigger safeguards?

Nuclear facilities are as a rule not supplied lock, stock and barrel. In most cases a large part of the construction is done locally with local materials, and only some

---

[14] Subsequently, the governments of the German Democratic Republic, Hungary and Poland made similar declarations.

[15] See appendix 1, Annex 1.

items of equipment and the designs for the plant are supplied from outside [9 c]. In addition, the supplier of the plant may train the recipient's staff and make engineers available for the construction of the facility. This point is not covered in Article III.2 of the NPT and, although the "trigger list" is not meant to be exhaustive, it is apparently not intended to cover know-how in any form, except perhaps as part of the supply of the items listed. On the other hand, it is highly likely that at least some suppliers of this kind of know-how will wish to assure themselves that it is not used for any military purpose and will therefore require the conclusion of a safeguards agreement. In this connection, it may be useful to refer to the IAEA Statute, which authorizes the Agency, *inter alia*, to establish and administer safeguards designed to ensure not only that materials and equipment are not used for any military purpose but also that "information made available by the Agency or at its request or under its supervision or control" is not used for the wrong purposes [2 d]. In fact, the last word in this respect must be with the supplier of the information. If he wishes that the technical data and experience he imparts should trigger safeguards he should make sure that the recipient goes to the Agency for a safeguards agreement.

The decision by the supplier states may, in the long run, have perceptible consequences on the Agency's safeguards task. As far as the major exporters on the nuclear market are concerned, it is not likely to add much to the Agency's work. Suppliers, such as Canada, the UK and the USA, which have been exporting the principal components of reactors, along with the fuel therefor, have done so largely by virtue of bilateral agreements for cooperation, the safeguards of which were transferred to the Agency. France has recently done the same [10]. Some other participants of the group already had the practice of requiring that states receiving major components and fuel for reactors should unilaterally submit these to safeguards. It is likely, however, that with the growing nuclear construction programmes that will soon be under way in various parts of the world, the supplies, particularly of equipment, by some of the smaller producer nations among those participating in the group's work will begin to attract safeguards on an increasing scale.

These arrangements pertain to exports in cases where the recipient state is not a party to the NPT. The safeguards referred to in these arrangements are those of the Safeguards System of 1965, with the clear understanding that the assurance to be rendered by this system pertains to the non-diversion of nuclear materials to any nuclear explosive device, whether military or not.[16] Although no overt declaration exists to this effect, it appears that the phrase "the safeguards required by this article" of Article III.2 has so far been taken by supplier states to mean "Agency safeguards" in the sense of both INFCIRC/153 and INFCIRC/66/Rev. 2; where the recipient is not a party to the NPT, safeguards pursuant to the latter document have been considered adequate. (The Agency's policy on duration and termination of the agreements under the Safeguards System of 1965, described here under the heading "Pursuit", is naturally closely connected with the implementation of this provision of the NPT.)

There is, of course, an anomaly in the fact that states not party to the NPT may

[16] See "Peaceful uses" above, pp. 10–13.

nevertheless continue to receive supplies of nuclear material and equipment, and at the price of safeguards that are less comprehensive than those accepted by the non-nuclear-weapon states party to the treaty.[17] There are good arguments for the case that supplier states should demand adherance to the NPT—and thus also to safeguards on the entire peaceful fuel cycle—as a condition for the delivery of nuclear material. It seems that the US government has accepted these arguments or is at least tending that way. Recent press reports mention that, in connection with the supply of nuclear facilities to Egypt and Israel, the USA would expect these states to put all their future nuclear activities under IAEA Safeguards [11]; this could be an eventual precedent for a US policy of making it a condition for all future supplies of this kind that recipient states should be parties to the NPT or at least agree to place all their atomic facilities under safeguards. These reports do not make it clear which of the two safeguards documents would be expected to govern such overall submissions. One also wonders what will happen where there are already agreements on such supplies. The USA is a party to a considerable number of agreements for cooperation in the field of nuclear energy, including the supply of nuclear material, equipment and facilities with non-nuclear-weapon states that are not or are not yet parties to the NPT. Such agreements provide for safeguards, but these are limited in scope to the items supplied. Presumably the USA cannot disregard these commitments. Recent extensions of several cooperation agreements and of the connected safeguards transfer agreements would seem to indicate that the USA is not planning in the short term to change its policy of supplying non-parties to the NPT with whom such agreements exist.

The question of the standards to which a safeguards agreement with the Agency has to conform, so that the procedures for which it provides qualify to serve, in terms of Article III.2, as "the safeguards required by this Article", leads to much discussion. It is connected with the entire problem of standardization and non-discrimination. NPT type agreements are standardized, but the agreements concluded under the Agency Safeguards System of 1965 differ among each other, *inter alia* in respect of provisions for duration and continuation of safeguards on produced special fissionable material [5 e]. INFCIRC/66/Rev. 2 provides that "appropriate provisions of this document" may be incorporated in bilateral and multilateral arrangements between states, "including all those that provide for the transfer to the Agency of responsibility for administering safeguards" [5 d]. It adds that the Agency will not assume such responsibility unless the principles of safeguards and the procedures to be used are "essentially consistent" with those of the document. There is a possible contradiction in this injunction. The word "appropriate" implies that one may choose from among procedures, whereas it would seem that to be "essentially consistent" the agreement must at least conform to certain standards of the document. There is no indication of the minimum requirements for this "consistency", and thus the door is open for departures from the norm.

This raises problems. Unless the Secretariat is given a clear mandate to negotiate

[17] This anomaly is cogently described in Goldblat, J., "The Indian Test and the NPT", paper presented at the Non-Proliferation Treaty "Preview" Conference, organized by the Arms Control Association and the Carnegie Endowment for International Peace, at Divonne, France, 9–11 September 1974.

only on the basis of a standardized text—as it does for agreements in connection with the NPT—it will find itself in a difficult position when negotiating safeguards agreements in respect of supplies of nuclear material and equipment by a third state. As a rule, such agreements are prompted by the fact that it is the supplier state which requires that safeguards should be applied in connection with such supplies, either as a consequence of its adherence to the NPT, to meet its obligations under Article III.2 or pursuant to its export policy. As has been seen, a number of supplier states, wishing to avoid unfairly competitive situations, have agreed on minimum requirements to be set in this respect. In so doing, they have *de facto* set standards for the safeguards which could qualify as being "required by this Article". The purchasing country, however, (which is probably not a party to the NPT, otherwise it would not now have to enter into negotiations on a safeguards agreement), is not directly involved and may not be particularly interested in helping the supplying country to comply with its obligations or its policy. As experience has shown, the purchaser will negotiate for the best possible conditions, taking the attitude that the unilateral submission is a voluntary move and that all it needs to do is to agree with the Agency on arrangements that are "essentially consistent" with those of the Agency's Safeguards System of 1965.

Although this is theoretically correct, it leaves the Agency's Secretariat facing a difficult situation: it is, in fact, negotiating with two countries, one of which remains in the shadows. One might say that, to some extent, the Agency's Secretariat has to comply with the wishes of supplier states, in having to conclude agreements that reach standards set by these suppliers. This is obviously the corollary of the policy of suppliers to demand safeguards against the misuse of the items they provide, while divesting themselves of at least part of the responsibility for doing so by charging the Agency with the application of safeguards. It is understandable that one can sometimes hear the accusation levelled at the Secretariat that it takes the side of the "haves"; this is as understandable as it is unavoidable. It would be a great help to the Secretariat if the Board of Governors were to decide—as it has in the case of NPT agreements—on a standard text for the appropriate agreements. Indeed, if at some time in the future all exporting states were to accept a unified policy of making it a condition of supply that recipient states submit all their peaceful nuclear activities to safeguards, a completely standardized approach would be essential, both to avoid discrimination and for operational reasons. INFCIRC/153 has shown the way in this respect.

VI. *Termination*

In this complex of concepts the question of termination of the agreement plays a large role. Its relevance in the context of export conditions is clear: in principle, safeguards should be applied for as long as the supplied item which "triggered" them and the special fissionable material produced by means of it remains in use. In its attempt to standardize, the Board of Governors has established the desirability of having agreements last for as long as the exported equipment or material is in use, but if the agreement is terminated earlier, safeguards should continue and "pursue" the produced material, generation after generation.

This rule—which will become all the more important as "breeder" reactors (which both produce and use large amounts of special fissionable material) come under safeguards—is valid not only for the "unilateral submission agreements" between a state and the Agency, by means of which third states are enabled to live up to their obligations under Article III.2 of the NPT, or to their own export policies. It is also valid in respect of "safeguards transfer agreements", through which two states party to an agreement for cooperation in the field of nuclear energy charge the Agency with the responsibility for applying safeguards. Normally, such safeguards transfer agreements are valid for the term of the bilateral cooperation agreement, "as extended or amended from time to time"; any party may terminate them on six months' notice. A number of these agreements provide for continuation of safeguards on produced material.[18] Others omit direct reference to continuation, but in such cases it is the rule that the Director General's memorandum, with which the draft agreement is submitted to the Board of Governers for approval, mentions that the governments concerned have expressed a willingness to consult on continuation of safeguards on produced material, should the agreement come to an end. It should be noted that in the event of a safeguards transfer agreement coming to an end other than by expiry of the bilateral agreement for cooperation underlying it, the bilateral safeguards would be resumed.

Safeguards agreements in connection with the NPT provide that they will remain in force as long as the state is a party to that treaty.[19] The treaty is to remain in force for 25 years; at that time a conference should decide on its continuation [6 b]. Thus, the pertinent safeguards agreements should also remain in force for an equal period. However, if a state makes use of its right to withdraw from the treaty: the safeguards agreement would come to an end then and there [6 c]. Many NPT agreements provide for the suspension of the application of Agency safeguards in the state under other safeguards agreements with the Agency, as long as safeguards are applied in connection with the NPT.[20] Once the state abrogates the latter agreement, safeguards under other agreements would be resumed. This could mean that, *inter alia*, the amounts of nuclear material present in the state (which under the NPT regime were all accounted for together in a unified inventory—without regard to origin) [3 e] should somehow be reallocated to different accounts, according to origin. Presumably, some method of prorating would be called for, by means of which not only quantities supplied directly from various sources, but also nuclear material produced by the use of supplied materials could be attributed to the original suppliers.

---

[18] The standard clause in such cases is "However, this Agreement shall remain in force with regard to any nuclear material referred to (in the Sub-Section regarding the entry in the inventory of special fissionable material produced in or by the use of supplied material, equipment or facilities) until the Agency has notified both Governments that it has terminated safeguards on such material . . ."

[19] Agreements concluded in connection with both the NPT and the Treaty of Tlatelolco remain in force as long as the state is a party to either treaty.

[20] Suspension is effected by means of a protocol concluded at the time of the conclusion of the NPT safeguards agreement, between the parties to the initial safeguards agreement. For instance, the protocol suspending a safeguards transfer agreement is concluded between the two Governments concerned and the Agency. The protocols are published in the Agency's "INFCIRC" series, as modifications to the original agreements.

So far this has been a hypothetical case, but if it should ever come to pass it will cause serious accounting problems both for the state concerned and for the Agency. If any state should denounce the NPT without rejecting Agency safeguards on its peaceful nuclear activities (that is, if it were to abrogate the NPT without taking the "nuclear option") one solution might be for the state to conclude a unilateral submission agreement covering all its peaceful nuclear activities, but outside the framework of the NPT. This has been done once, in the case of Panama, but that agreement was concluded pursuant to Article 13 of the Treaty of Tlatelolco. Whether the Board would ever approve an NPT-type submission agreement with a state that is not a party to any multilateral arrangement of the NPT/Tlatelolco kind cannot be predicted.

References

1. Rometsch, R. "Development of IAEA Safeguards System for NPT", Paper No. A/CONF.49/P/770, presented at the Fourth UN International Conference on the Peaceful Uses of Atomic Energy, Geneva, September 1971.
2. IAEA Statute
   (a) ——, Article XII.C.
   (b) ——, Article XI.F.4.
   (c) ——, Article XII.A.5. as quoted in INFCIRC/66/Rev. 2 paragraph 16.
   (d) ——, Article III.A.5.
3. INFCIRC/153.
   (a) ——, paragraph 18.
   (b) ——, paragraph 19.
   (c) ——, paragraphs 1 and 28.
   (d) ——, paragraph 6(c).
   (e) ——, paragraph 41.
4. Statement by the Minister for External Affairs of India on 21 May 1974, reproduced in document CCD/425.
5. INFCIRC/66/Rev. 2.
   (a) ——, paragraph 82.
   (b) ——, paragraph 3.
   (c) ——, paragraph 4.
   (d) ——, paragraph 5.
   (e) ——, paragraph 16.
6. Non-Proliferation Treaty.
   (a) ——, Hearing before the Committee on Foreign Relations, United States Senate, 90th Congress (Washington: US Government Printing Office, 1968), p. 39. (See also "Arms Limitation Agreements—July 1974 Summit; Publication No. 73 of the US Arms Control and Disarmament Agency, for a more recent reflection on this viewpoint.)
   (b) ——, Article X.2.
   (c) ——, Article X.1.
7. *Nature*, Vol. 249. 31 May 1974, p. 397.
8. *Documentation*, (Brussels, International Law Association, and Karlsruhe, Gesellschaft für Kernforschung MBH).
   (a) ——, p. 383.
   (b) ——, p. 385.
9. Szasz, Paul C., "The Law and Practices of the International Atomic Energy Agency". Vienna, IAEA Legal Series No. 7, 1970.
   (a) ——, paragraphs 21.5.4.3. and 21.6.2.2. *et seq.*

(b) ——, paragraphs 21.6.1.3., 21.6.2.1.1., and 21.6.227.

(c) ——, p. 587.

10. INFCIRC/171.

11. See also Finney, J.W., "Inspection Sought in US Atom Offer", *New York Times*, 2 October 1974, as quoted in *International Herald Tribune*, 3 October 1974.

3. The application

I. *Subsidiary arrangements*

The so-called Subsidiary Arrangements are an important element in the standardization of the application of the safeguards procedures.

The Safeguards System of 1965 lists a number of principles which should govern the application of safeguards. It also lists general procedures regarding the main types of installations with which the Agency is involved. It could not, however, set out the detailed practices to be applied in each specific case. Particularly with respect to record keeping and reporting, it was left to the Agency and the state concerned to work out in detail for each facility — for instance, what information would be kept and made available and how often reports would be made. The agreements made pursuant to the older document are also not the most suitable instruments in which to incorporate technical rules and arrangements of this kind; moreover, such arrangements should be susceptible to easy adaptation to changed circumstances and should therefore lend themselves to relatively frequent changes. Therefore, it became the practice to incorporate such detailed procedures in Subsidiary Arrangements, which are usually in the form of letters exchanged between the Agency's Secretariat and the governmental authority involved. Some agreements made pursuant to the Safeguards System of 1965 make specific references to the conclusion of Subsidiary Arrangements; in others these are not mentioned but they have, in fact, been concluded wherever Agency safeguards are applied. Typically, they include the definition of each facility involved; the records system; the reports system; procedures for exemption of nuclear materials from safeguards and for suspension of safeguards; rules for the steps to be taken before safeguarded nuclear material may be transferred to facilities where previously no safeguards were applied, and specific safeguards measures of the Agency, such as the use of surveillance cameras and the taking of samples. Even though, as stated before, the agreement under the Safeguards System of 1965 might vary, the Subsidiary Arrangements tend to reflect as fas as possible standardized procedures. This standardization process is helped by the fact that, for instance in a non-NPT state with which there is more than one type of agreement, the Agency tries to conclude a single set of Subsidiary Arrangements covering all its safeguards activities there.

Subsidiary Arrangements were first worked out when the application of agreements concluded under the Safeguards System of 1965 was found to require the elaboration of more precise rules than were provided by the basic documents. As a result, they at first had a rather amorphous character. The "Blue Book" on the other hand, which gives the contents of the agreements to be concluded under the NPT, makes specific provision for the conclusion of Subsidiary Arrangements [1 a]. This enabled the Secretariat to elaborate from the beginning the Subsidiary Arrangements to the NPT type safeguards agreements. In so doing it could ensure that all agreements could be applied in a standardized fashion, *viz.*, that wherever circumstances are similar, the same safeguards treatment is applied.

The safeguards relations between the Agency and any state are therefore governed not only by the safeguards agreement but also by the Subsidiary Arrangements that give the technical and administrative details of safeguards implementation which cannot be found in the agreement. On the other hand, the Subsidiary Arrangements carefully avoid giving the Agency any rights that are not found in the underlying agreement. A Subsidiary Arrangement may elaborate and specify; it does not add. At times, the negotiation of Subsidiary Arrangements (in which, as a rule, the participants on the government side are facility operators, employees of the state accounting and control system and lower level administrators, rather than primarily officials of the Foreign Ministry, as in the case of the agreement itself) is more arduous than the discussions on the underlying agreement. This is not surprising. Once the actual implementation begins, it is the Subsidiary Arrangements that are consulted by the staff on the working level and applied on the shop-floor. Careful agreement on the day-to-day application pays off in terms of subsequent good practical relations. It is the Agency's experience that the understandings reached during the discussions on the Subsidiary Arrangements can greatly facilitate the application of safeguards.

The Subsidiary Arrangements consist of a "General Part" and one "Attachment" for each facility and for nuclear material outside facilities. The General Part contains the rules and procedures that are applicable to all facilities and for the country as a whole. Among other things it specifies channels to be followed in communicating on safeguards matters between the government and the Agency; gives details of the national system of accounting for and control of nuclear material; sets the dates and time limits for the provision of information to the Agency, including the various accounting reports and advance notifications on international transfers; specifies what statements are made by the Agency to the state and when, and lists what summarized information may be published by the Agency on the application of safeguards in the state.[1] The General Part further contains a series of models for the communications to be exchanged on termination of and exemption from safeguards, for the advance notification on exports and imports of safeguarded material, for the inspection assignments to be used by the Agency, for the periodic inspection programme which it should communicate. An essential section in the General Part of the Subsidiary Arrangements is made up of the *pro formas* of the accounting reports to be submitted by the state and the detailed explanation on how these should be completed. The General Part may also include arrangements for the presentation and transmission of accounting data in a form directly suitable for electronic data processing.

The Attachment that is prepared for each facility containing safeguarded nuclear material firstly identifies that facility and gives a precise description of it. It is based on the design information submitted by the state and is naturally changed as and when modifications of such design information are received. The modifications on which information is to be given in advance, because they will have an impact on the safeguards procedures to be applied, are specified in the attachments. The attachment sets out the way the basic measure of accountancy is to be applied. It

[1] In these remarks and in the remainder of this section, reference is made primarily to Subsidiary Arrangements pursuant to agreements concluded in connection with the NPT.

specifies material balance areas[2] in which the facility may be divided or, if for reasons of safeguards practice the facility is part of a material balance area which comprises several installations, it describes that arrangement. Under "accountancy" the "strategic points" are specified; first, where the flow of nuclear material through the facility is determined and, second, where the physical inventory is determined. Procedures are also given for the verification of the physical inventory taking. In respect of the measures of "containment" and "surveillance" the strategic points are indicated where such measures may be applied, and the instruments and devices to be used are listed. In connection with record keeping and reporting the facility attachment specifies for each "key measurement point" (that is, for each location where nuclear material appears in such a form that it may be measured to determine material flow or inventory) what data have to be recorded and reported. The timing and form of the reporting of the various items is specified. Further, the attachment gives an indication of the actual inspection effort to be made at the facility by the Agency, as long as the situation there is as described in the relevant information. The scope of the routine inspections is also indicated. The attachment contains a series of detailed administrative arrangements for such items as the contacts to be maintained at the facility, the services to be provided by the facility operator in connection with the Agency's inspections and the charges to be made therefor as well as the way in which these would be reimbursed. Lastly, specifications are given of the statements the Agency is required to make on the result of these inspections and on the conclusions it draws from its verification activities.

Each facility attachment is based on a model worked out by the Agency's Secretariat for the type of facility concerned and is modified to take account of the specific circumstances at hand. The facility attachment should be agreed upon in the minutest detail by the operator and the state's authorities on the one hand and the Secretariat on the other. This process of agreement may involve a clash of interests. The Agency is concerned to apply safeguards as well as possible, using experience obtained elsewhere, and to make all attachments for the type of facility as uniform as possible. It has to standardize. The state and the operator, of course, wish to reduce the safeguards burden to a minimum. They are interested in ensuring that they are not discriminated against, but their concern for the concept of standardization need not go beyond this point. The Agency continuously gains experience in its safeguards application and wishes to reflect this in facility attachments, whereas the persons negotiating for the state may propose amendments that both meet their own interests and satisfy those of the Agency. The resulting agreed facility attachments may well deviate from the model, so that the standard is departed from. Often such departures are improvements. States that have already agreed on facility attachments conforming to the previous standard have the right to benefit from such improvements. Consequently, the Agency's Secretariat is involved in a continuous process of negotiation and renegotiation of facility attachments. The end of this process is not yet in sight. It is tempting to call for a cut-off point, beyond which improvements can no longer be incorporated in standard documents. Common sense rejects this, however, and the practical application of safeguards will in the long run greatly benefit from a flexible attitude of the Agency in this respect.

[2] See page 36.

II. *The role of the nuclear-weapon states*

The interest of most of the nuclear-weapon states in non-proliferation measures is obvious. The United States was the first active promoter of international safeguards. The United Kingdom also actively supported Agency safeguards from the moment these were under debate. The Soviet Union joined in at a later stage. In 1959 agreements were concluded between the IAEA on the one hand and the governments of the USSR, UK and USA on the other, under which these states made available to the Agency various quantities of nuclear material. Only the agreements with the UK and the USA made specific mention of the application of safeguards in connection with this material [2]. From the moment that they started to supply nuclear material and equipment to third states both governments have insisted on safeguards, and as soon as the IAEA had established a suitable safeguards system they transferred their bilateral safeguards arrangements to the Agency. In 1961 the United States invited the Agency to apply its safeguards for a limited period to four of its reactors to permit testing and development of the Agency's safeguards procedures on actual reactor installations of various types [3]. The relevant agreement, which covered four research or experimental reactors, entered into force on 1 June 1962 and the first inspections were begun at once. In 1964 this agreement was replaced by one providing for the safeguarding of a US nuclear power station and for continuing safeguards on three of the reactors previously covered [4]. In June 1965 the United Kingdom announced that it was prepared to place the Bradwell nuclear power station under Agency safeguards for purposes of development of procedures and familiarization with this type of facility. The relevant agreement entered into force on 1 September 1966 [5]. It has since expired. However, there is an agreement in force between the Agency and the United Kingdom (INFCIRC/175) under which Agency safeguards are applied in respect of nuclear material in Britain, which is covered by safeguards transfer agreements and is returned to that country for reprocessing.

The Agency was also enabled to carry out safeguards operations in respect of nuclear material from the US power station mentioned above, both while the material was being reprocessed and later when it was stored in facilities elsewhere, and also in respect of plutonium in a fast experimental facility in the United Kingdom, which had been substituted for the plutonium produced in and later extracted from the Bradwell fuel. With the increased interest of the USSR in Agency safeguards, this country has also on several occasions made facilities available to Agency safeguards staff, enabling them to acquaint themselves with this type of plant and learn safeguards procedures applicable to it. These three nuclear-weapon states have done a large amount of development work for the Agency in the area of safeguards and are continuing to do so. They also both develop, and enable the Agency to test, various safeguards devices.

France has never shown public enthusiasm for international safeguards. It did participate in the various working groups and committees of the Agency for the preparation of its several safeguards documents. On the other hand, by insisting repeatedly that costs of safeguards, particularly under safeguards transfer agreements, should be borne by the governments party to these agreements, France seemed to illustrate its view that these kinds of safeguards should not receive an undue weight among the Agency's activities. Lately, however, the French attitude to safeguards seems to have undergone some change. France became party to a safeguards transfer agreement with Japan, concluded in the first place in connection with the supply by France to Japan of a large reprocessing installation [6]. France appears to have been instrumental in the unilateral submission by Spain of enriched uranium of French origin fabricated there for, and supplied to, Chile where it will also be under Agency safeguards. Although France is not a party to the NPT it has publicly declared that it intends to ensure that its exports of nuclear material and equipment should not contribute to the proliferation of nuclear weapons.[3]

In December 1967, during a meeting of what was then still the Eighteen-Nation Committee on Disarmament, the governments of the United Kingdom and the United States announced that, once international safeguards were put into effect in the non-nuclear-weapon states in implementation of the provisions of the NPT they would permit the IAEA to apply its safeguards in their two countries, subject to certain restrictions. The declaration of the United Kingdom [7 a] contained the phrase that the government would be prepared to "offer an opportunity for the application of similar safeguards in the United Kingdom subject to exclusions for national security reasons only". The US president said that his country would "permit the International Atomic Energy Agency to apply its safeguards to all nuclear activities in the United States—excluding only those with direct national security significance" [7 b]. These offers were made primarily to facilitate the acceptance of the NPT by the more highly developed non-nuclear-weapon states, by imposing on the nuclear-weapon states the same presumed commercial disadvantages—referred to colloquially as "equality of misery"—as would have to be borne by other states in accepting international safeguards. At the time of writing, negotiations between the Agency and the United Kingdom and the United States are going on for the implementation of the offers.

There is, of course, no obligation in the NPT for nuclear-weapon states to accept safeguards on their peaceful nuclear activities [8 a].[4] The submission to safeguards of peaceful nuclear activities in states which in any case dispose of a mighty nuclear arsenal is considered in some quarters to be of no direct significance to the cause of non-proliferation. On the other hand, it is obvious that the nuclear-weapon states have to play an important role under the NPT in the context of safeguards in non-nuclear-weapon states, both as suppliers of nuclear material to such states and as recipients. No international system of safeguards is complete unless the safeguarding authority is aware of international shipments of nuclear material and can receive confirmation both from the shipping and the receiving end, whether the

---

[3] At the resumed twenty-second session of the United Nations General Assembly, where the report of the Eighteen-Nation Committee on Disarmament, including the draft of the NPT, was discussed, France stated that although it would not sign the treaty it would behave in the future exactly as the States adhering to it.

[4] Under the Safeguards System of (1965) the obligation to accept safeguards may arise if, for instance, nuclear material is returned to a nuclear-weapon state that originally supplied it and this material is "improved"—that is, the concentration of fissionable isotopes in it has been increased—as is for instance the case in irradiated natural uranium, which contains plutonium [8a].

states involved are non-nuclear-weapon or nuclear-weapon states. The need for the Agency to be aware of such movements was highlighted in a number of statements by non-nuclear-weapon states [9], at the ninth General Conference of the IAEA, in 1965. In that year the United States reached agreements with the governments and international organizations to which it supplied nuclear materials, whereby the USA would register semi-annually with the Agency all transfers of nuclear material under such agreements which were not reported to the Agency pursuant to safeguards agreements. The director general followed up the suggestions made at the General Conference by consulting with the principal suppliers of nuclear materials concerning the possibility of setting up a system for reporting and registering of international transfers of such material. In response, the governments of Canada and Norway undertook to inform the Agency of their exports of nuclear material; they continued to do so, until their agreements with the Agency in connection with the NPT entered into force (which made it anyway incumbent upon them to inform the Agency of such exports and imports).

In drafting the document on the structure and content of agreements between the Agency and states required in connection with the NPT, the Safeguards Committee realized that the information available to the Agency would be incomplete unless the nuclear-weapon states that receive nuclear material from non-nuclear-weapon states can somehow be involved; the Agency would never be in a position to confirm that the nuclear material reported to be shipped had, in fact, left the non-nuclear-weapon state. Nuclear-weapon states could not be bound to confirm that they had indeed received material that had been under safeguards in the shipping state. Accordingly, the drafters of the document included a provision that, in the case of such a shipment, the exporting state should make arrangements for the Agency to receive confirmation from the recipient state of the transfer [1 b].

The three depository powers have since gone further. In June 1974 the governments of the United Kingdom, the Soviet Union and the United States agreed to assist the Agency in its safeguards activities by providing it henceforth with information on anticipated exports and imports of nuclear material. In identical letters dated 10 July 1974 [10] these governments undertook to provide the Agency on a continuing basis with advance information on the export of nuclear material, in an amount exceeding one effective kilogram for peaceful purposes to any non-nuclear-weapon state, afterwards providing confirmation of each export. They would also inform the Agency of each import of more than one effective kilogram of nuclear material which, immediately prior to export from the shipping state, was subject to safeguards under an agreement with the Agency. This latter formulation was presumably designed to avoid having to report on the import of material that had not yet reached the stage where safeguards applied to it [1 c]; it may be imagined that imports take place of such material, intended for the military programmes of the states concerned. The Agency was advised that the provision of this information would be initiated no later than 1 October 1974. This is an important contribution to the establishment of a truly worldwide safeguards system. It is, of course, limited to the three countries concerned, but together these account for a large part of the nuclear market, both as consumers and producers. It may be assumed that the greater part of the transactions between non-nuclear-weapon states is known anyway, because the material involved is subject to safeguards at both ends. Naturally, as international trade in nuclear material increases between states that have not accepted safeguards obligations, or whose safeguards obligations are limited in scope and do not extend to such transactions, more and more of these transfers are likely to escape beyond the ken of the Agency. But the international community should be aware, at least in general lines, of the magnitude and scope of the nuclear effort of all its members. It is therefore of further great importance that all powers, and not only the three nuclear ones mentioned above, and the non-nuclear-weapon states that have not accepted safeguards on all their peaceful nuclear activities, should adhere to the scheme suggested in 1965.

III. *Physical protection*

The safeguards so far discussed here as envisaged in the various non-proliferation measures are all intended to detect diversion of nuclear material to prohibited purposes, by governments. Of possibly equal importance is the question of diversion on a sub-governmental level: theft of nuclear material or sabotage of installations by individuals or non-governmental groups, for purposes ranging from personal economic gain to political blackmail. This problem has recently come into the focus of public interest [11]. The protection of nuclear material and facilities against illegal acts is an essential supplement to any safeguards system based on accountancy. Such safeguards can *detect* the disappearance of nuclear material; physical security measures have to be taken to *prevent* such disappearance and to *recover* material that has gone astray.

Neither the Agency's Statute nor the Safeguards System of 1965 or the "Blue Book" mentions the physical protection of nuclear material among the Agency's safeguards tasks.[5] It is clear that the establishment and implementation of a physical protection system within the state is the responsibility of that state and should go in parallel with and be closely connected to the establishment of the state's national system of accounting for and control of nuclear material. The existence of an adequate system of physical security is one condition for the credibility of the national accounting and control system. This means that the adequacy of the physical protection measures taken by a state helps to determine the effectiveness of the Agency's safeguards. The responsibility for physical protection of nuclear material in international transfer is a matter for agreement between the states concerned. This point may be even more important internationally than the physical security on the sub-national level because an act of sabotage or theft on, say, the high seas may cause immediate international problems. But, indirectly, sub-national diversion may also become a problem of international security——namely, if diverted nuclear material were to be transferred to a foreign government for purposes of its own. Without involving diversion on the national

---

[5] Article XII.A.5. of the Statute, which gives the Agency the right to require deposit with it of excess special fissionable material "to prevent stockpiling of these materials" might be interpreted as a measure of physical security to be taken by the Agency. It has never been implemented and is not mentioned in either of the Agency's safeguards documents.

level, such an act might still lead to proliferation of nuclear military capacity [12]. The question of physical protection. therefore, is closely connected with the purpose of international safeguards.

There is increasing international interest in the Agency's role in this area. The Agency has so far played a relatively minor part. In 1971 and 1972 it convened a group of consultants and sponsored a panel of experts, which resulted in a set of recommendations on the physical protection of nuclear material. These recommendations, published in the so-called "Grey Book" of June 1972, are of a rather general nature. Whereas the actual protective measures can be decided upon only in the light of concrete circumstance and must be taken nationally, or perhaps regionally, the Agency might well step up its advisory work in this respect. During the last General Conference a number of delegates called on the IAEA to do so, and, among other things, to give guidance to states on minimum standards for physical protection of special fissionable material, possibly to be codified in an international agreement. It was suggested that the Agency should continue on an increased scale to compile experiences and suggestions from states that are most active in this field, and make the results available. There were also calls for the Agency to give advice, upon request, on the quality of operation of national physical security systems and assist states to improve their capability in this area.

To these proposals one might add the suggestion that the Agency's statements on the technical conclusions of safeguards which the NPT-type agreements oblige the Agency to make to the state[6] could, if the state so wished, be supplemented by a statement on the conclusions drawn from observation of the state's physical security measures.

Also, at the last regular session of the General Conference there was general agreement with the director general's suggestion that the Agency had a role to play in the elaboration of rules for the international transport of special fissionable material. The conference also heard suggestions for studies on the siting of various activities in the fuel cycle so as to minimize the risk of theft or sabotage [13]. Evidently, the international community has become aware that international safeguards are closely connected with national and, indeed, international measures of physical security.

IV. *The two safeguards documents*

This section attempts to show some of the aspects in which document INFCIRC/153 differs from INFCIRC/66/Rev. 2—both being documents that contain "the Agency's safeguards system", but the former much further developed, with a particular view to serving under the circumstances envisaged in the NPT: with all peaceful nuclear activities of a state being covered by the Agency's safeguards. Completeness is not intended here. A full exposé of the virtues and vices of one document as against the other involves many technical and political elements and would go beyond the scope of this volume. Moreover, INFCIRC/153 was not only intended as an improvement over INFCIRC/66 but it was meant to be used

---

[6] See page 8.

under different circumstances. A comparison in-depth can therefore never be entirely valid. If present appearances do not deceive, both documents may have to be applied alongside each other, for an indefinite time. While this will cause some practical difficulties for the Agency, these will not be insoluble.

Both documents contain the basic injunction that safeguards should not be detrimental to the development and use of peaceful nuclear activities, and provide that safeguards shall be implemented in a manner designed to avoid hampering the economic and technical development of the state or international cooperation in the field of nuclear activities, including international exchange of nuclear material. Both also stipulate that the safeguards should be consistent with prudent management practices required for the economic and safe conduct of nuclear activities. It is the aim of the Secretariat to apply its safeguards procedures under either document impartially and objectively. Its very conscious efforts at avoiding any discrimination are described elsewhere in this paper.[7] As its experience grows, the Secretariat feels it has grounds to believe that the existence of international safeguards operated on the basis of these principles is becoming a positive factor in the development of nuclear energy, particularly in that it encourages states to engage in international trade, or to sanction such trade by their national companies, where they might feel constraints in doing so without safeguards.

The warning contained in Article III.3 of the NPT that safeguards should not become an undue burden has been a guiding principle for the Agency ever since it started its safeguarding task. The very wording of that article seems to have been derived from the Agency's Safeguards System of 1965. This "burden" has been a point of discussion throughout the debate on the NPT. The Agency's experience shows that much of the preoccupation with a possible negative impact of safeguards has been caused by ignorance of the actual practices. It has, however, led to the introduction into INFCIRC/153 of a great deal of what might be called "refinement", as compared to INFCIRC/66/Rev. 2. The latter is an open-ended document: it does not limit the access for inspection purposes in a facility; it leaves a great deal of flexibility in respect of the frequency with which inspections can be made; and, in allowing the Agency much freedom in its choice of the mode of application of safeguards, it may not always give the operator a complete picture in advance of the safeguards treatment he should be expected to receive at the hands of the Agency. In fact, as shown elsewhere in this volume, the Subsidiary Arrangements contain the detail the operator needs in order to know his precise rights and obligations, and one has seen that in practice the application leads to a minimum of problems. There have been a few occasions when an operator has considered that the presence of Agency inspectors during a period of particularly hectic operations was somewhat disturbing. In such cases it has been possible to reach agreement on the use of optical surveillance equipment which made it feasible to minimize the intrusiveness of inspection.

A subject much discussed in recent years has been the supposed danger that industrial secrets would come into the hands of unauthorized persons, through safeguards. Here again, practice has shown that such fears were exaggerated. In the first place few, if any, of the installations so far visited have been of an entirely new

[7] See p. 14.

character. Much information the Agency requires is only that which is directly connected with the application of safeguards and is, more often than not, of a general nature. The technology of the manufacture of mechanical components, for instance, or the materials used in their fabrication, are details of great commercial sensitivity which would be of no interest to the Agency. The "Blue Book" prescribes the purposes for which design information may be examined and also stipulates that the Agency shall examine such information on the state's premises if the state so wishes. If there is a step in the process which involves commercially sensitive information, the state may request to have this part excluded from the verification process. In such a case, the Agency will, if possible, try to obtain the picture of the material flow and inventory of the plant while bypassing the sensitive area. So far, this has been possible also because, if the operator wishes to have part of his process closed to inspection, he will see to it that he compensates for this by enabling the Agency to get an overall picture of the activities of the installation through information obtained elsewhere——for example, at the input and at the end of the sensitive zone.

The precise provisions in the "Blue Book" for the kind of design information to be made available and the purposes for which it may be examined constitute one point of difference between the two documents. Both documents state that the Agency must take every precaution to protect commercial and industrial secrets and other confidential information coming to its knowledge in the implementation of safeguards. Internal security measures to protect safeguards information have been in force in the Agency as long as safeguards have been applied. It is basically up to the governments to ear-mark information as being of particular sensitivity, and they should indicate this when they send such information to the Secretariat. This varies from state to state. Some states may not only classify information on the design of installations but also the accounting reports that may convey an idea of the capacity and the actual production of such installations. Other states may be less concerned about the confidential nature of the data they provide. The Secretariat follows the principle that certain categories of information should in any case be handled by the Agency with particular care, whether or not it is marked by the state as being of special sensitivity. Thus, there are basically two types of sensitive information: technical know-how which is not needed for safeguards purposes (this type of information the Agency tries to refrain from obtaining), and data on material flow and inventory, which is needed from the safeguards point of view, and may be commercially sensitive. This information the Agency does its best to protect.

Under agreements in connection with the NPT, safeguards are applied to all nuclear material in all peaceful nuclear activities of the state. The agreements concluded pursuant to the Agency's Safeguards System of 1965 normally pertain only to defined nuclear activities of the state, for example, a given Agency project, a specified facility submitted to Agency safeguards or, in the case of a safeguards transfer agreement, activities in which a particular third state is involved.[8]

---

[8] In one case an agreement concluded under INFCIRC/66/Rev.2 covered all nuclear activities in a state. This was the agreement with Mexico for the application of safeguards under the Treaty of Tlatelolco, published as INFCIRC/118. It was superseded by an agreement for the application of safeguards both in connection with the NPT and the Treaty of Tlatelolco, INFCIRC/197.

Safeguards in the former category are concerned only with verifying that there is no diversion of nuclear material to nuclear weapons or other nuclear explosive devices. The obligations of states party to agreements under INFCIRC/66/Rev.2 go further, in the sense that such agreements not only prohibit the use of the items covered for the development and manufacture of any nuclear explosive devices but also in any other activity that furthers a military purpose. When, upon the conclusion of an NPT agreement, an agreement under INFCIRC/66/Rev.2 is suspended, the undertaking not to further any military purpose remains valid.

An important and novel feature of the Agency's safeguards in connection with the NPT is the formal requirement for the state to establish and maintain a system of accounting for and control of all nuclear material subject to safeguards under the agreement. The "Blue Book" states that safeguards shall be applied in such a manner as to verify, in ascertaining that there has been no diversion, findings of the state's system [1 d]. The Agency's verification shall include, *inter alia*, independent measures and observations conducted in accordance with procedures that are laid down in the agreement in some detail. The Agency, in its verification, shall take due account of the technical effectiveness of the state's system.

The agreements provide that the Agency shall make full use of the national system and should avoid unnecessary duplication of the state's accounting and control activities [1 e]. The "Blue Book" describes some of the elements required of the national system [1 f]. These include, for example, a system for measuring quantities of nuclear material together with a system for evaluating the precision and accuracy of measurements; procedures for inventory-taking and evaluation of accumulations of unmeasured inventory and losses, a records and reports system, and measures to ensure that the accounting procedures are operated correctly. The specific situation in the country will of course determine to what extent some of the actions listed are taken by the plant operator or perhaps by the state authority itself. The national system of accounting for and control of nuclear material is in fact the infrastructure for the application of the international safeguards system [14 a]. The Safeguards System of 1965 makes no mention of the existence of a national accounting system. Obviously each state that has concluded a safeguards agreement with the Agency, also under that document, has to establish the internal machinery needed to meet its obligations under the agreement; there are no specific requirements for the organization of the system, however, and it is therefore left entirely up to the state to establish and run such a system.

Further, whereas under INFCIRC/153 the Agency's inspection effort may be influenced by the effectiveness of the national system and the quality of its findings, the Agency's inspection effort pursuant to INFCIRC/66/Rev.2 has no formal relationship with such activities of the state. The definition of the role of the state's system of accountancy and control is specific to the NPT agreements.

Besides providing a basis for the application of Agency safeguards, the national system will also have the task of guarding against diversion of nuclear material at the sub-national level and of taking appropriate measures to ensure the physical security of nuclear material. The functions of prevention of diversion and of eventual recovery of nuclear material that has gone astray logically belong to the national authorities; the Agency's task is primarily that of detection. It needs the cooperation with the national system in order that the required accounting data are made available as records, are open to inspection by the Agency and are transmitted to it in the form of reports. Further, the national system should evaluate this information. The extent to which there will be a national inspection apparatus will depend on the nature and size of the state's nuclear activities and the consequent degree of complexity of the state's accounting and control measures. The Agency does not yet have much experience regarding the extent to which a national system can be affiliated with international safeguards work. The protocol to the NPT agreement signed on 5 April 1973 by the Agency, the European Atomic Energy Community (Euratom) and the non-nuclear-weapon states that are members of Euratom contains provisions on the coordination of the safeguards activities of both organizations. Some of the technical elements of these coordination arrangements might also be relevant for the relationship between a highly developed national system and Agency safeguards, provided the national system meets a number of criteria. The most important of these would probably consist of standards and procedures for the acceptance or rejection of the operator's measurements and the way these are verified by the national system. The coordination arrangements between the Agency and Euratom are based in the first place on the existence of a technically effective and functionally independent control system susceptible to being adapted to meet the requirements resulting from the agreements. Provided that a state has a technically highly developed national system and is prepared to undertake substantial obligations in organizing and operating it, certain elements of the arrangements might also be relevant to agreements between individual states and the Agency. Such arrangements would have to enable the Agency to acquire full knowledge of the results obtained through national inspections, so that it can use these for its own verification while, of course, always having to be in a position to carry out substantial independent verification effort through direct access to all the information on which the findings of the national system are based [14 b].

The "Blue Book" states that the safeguards measure of fundamental importance is material accountancy, based on a system of so-called "Material Balance Areas" (MBA). This concept follows from the fact that the Agency is not concerned primarily with facilities as such but with the location and the flow of nuclear material. The material balance area is a functional device intended to facilitate material accountability; it is an area chosen so that all material entering or leaving it is measurable and in which the inventory of the material situated there can be determined. In short, it is a functional and geographic area where the material balance can be made up. The MBA can be part of a facility, it can be co-incident with a facility or it can consist of several facilities. The use of the concept permits safeguards to be concentrated on key measurement points where the flow or inventory of nuclear material may be determined. Under the material accountancy approach the Agency is informed, from records and by means of reports, of changes in the inventory of nuclear material in the material balance area. It can thus establish the book inventory for each such area and, by verifying that this is consistent with the actual situation, the Agency can detect possible diversion that might be hidden by falsified accountancy. Periodically, physical inventories are taken by the operator and verified by the Agency. The difference that may arise between the book inventory and the physical inventory at the end of a period for which the material balance is established is the so-called "material unaccounted for". The significance, in absolute and relative terms, of this amount, and its limits of error, serves as an indication as to whether diversion may be taking place and determines the need for any further action, including subsequent investigation. The Agency's verification activities can thus lead to the statement, in respect of each MBA on the amount of material unaccounted for in that area over a specific period and on the accuracy with which this amount is known.

Material accountancy is complemented by containment and surveillance measures. For containment, use is made of the structural features of the facility, amplified as appropriate by such devices as seals to ensure the actual presence of nuclear material where this is reported to be. Surveillance employs methods such as the use of unattended optical and other instruments to ascertain whether the material flow is as reported.

An important issue in the elaboration of INFCIRC/153 was the question at what stage in the fuel cycle safeguards would have to start. It was clearly felt to be undesirable as well as relatively useless to introduce control procedures in mining or ore-concentration work, among other reasons because uranium mining often goes hand-in-hand with the exploitation of other minerals which are of no relevance to nuclear safeguards. It was therefore decided to set the starting point for the application of safeguards at the stage in the fuel cycle where nuclear material reaches such purity and composition as to make it potentially suitable for nuclear use. However, material which has not reached that stage but is being exported to a non-nuclear-weapon state, or which is imported, should be reported to the Agency, unless it is destined for non-nuclear uses. The Safeguards System of 1965 does not indicate the point where nuclear material becomes susceptible to the application of safeguards procedures. It does, however, exempt mines and ore-processing plants from the facilities where safeguards procedures can be applied.

Under NPT-type agreements, when nuclear material is exported from the state, safeguards in respect of that material terminate as far as the state is concerned. A system of advance notifications and of reports is included to ensure that the Agency has knowledge of the destination of the exported material. Arrangements are also provided for confirmation of imports in cases where the material is not subject to safeguards in the recipient state. Steps recently announced by three nuclear-weapon states to keep the Agency abreast of imports and exports[9] will go far towards giving the Agency a complete picture of the international flow of nuclear material. Whereas Article III.2 indicates for the parties to the NPT the conditions under which exports can be made, the Safeguards System of 1965 had to include provisions both for the possibility of export of safeguarded items and the termination of safeguards in respect of such items. In respect of termination of safeguards by means of export it provides that such termination shall take place only if: (a) the material is being returned "unimproved" that is, without its fissile content being increased, to the state that originally supplied it, or (b) the material is transferred for given purposes and either does not exceed certain low quantitative limits or material is substituted for it for a limited period, or (c) arrangements have been made by the Agency to safeguard the material in the state to which it is being

9 See p. 30.

transferred, *or* (*d*) the material not being subject to safeguards pursuant to a project agreement, will be subject in the state to which it is being transferred to safeguards other than those of the Agency but generally consistent with such safeguards and accepted by the Agency.

The last of these four provisions has never been applied.[10] The third one, in fact, is very similar to the provision of Article III.2 of the NPT.

One of the major aspects in which INFCIRC/153 differs from INFCIRC/66/Rev.2 is in the definition of the purpose and scope of inspections. This is one of the more important ways in which the "open-endedness" of the Safeguards System of 1965, which has often been criticized, was ended in the NPT-type agreements.

INFCIRC/66/Rev.2, although describing the activities that may be included in routine inspections, lacks the precision of INFCIRC/153 in this respect. The latter document describes in detail for what purposes inspections may be made and what their scope shall be, that is, what activities may be undertaken by the inspector. Examples of these are the independent measurement of nuclear material, verification of the functioning and calibration of instruments, the application of surveillance measures, observation of sampling and measurement by the operator and a number of other activities. INFCIRC/66/Rev.2 contains no limitations on the access by inspectors to the facilities inspected; INFCIRC/153 limits routine inspections to strategic points that should be specified in the Subsidiary Arrangements, and to the records. Additional access is possible under special circumstances but only in agreement with the state.

Another limitation of inspections is contained in the *maxima* set by the two documents. Under INFCIRC/66/Rev.2 these *maxima* are predicated on the inventory of the facility, its throughput or its maximum potential annual production of special fissionable material, whichever is the largest. The maximum permissible number of routine inspections is in direct proportion to these figures. Where inventory, throughput or maximum production of special fissionable material is 60 kg or more the inspectors have the right of access at all times. The document gives some general rules for the determination of the actual frequency of inspection, but it does not limit the length of any single inspection nor does it give rules to take account of the participation of more than one inspector. INFCIRC/153, on the other hand, prescribes the *maxima*——in terms of man-years (*viz.* 300 man-days of inspection, a man-day being at day during which an inspector has access for a total of not more than eight hours)——which may be deployed at any one of a

---

[10] The Treaty of Rome, by which, *inter alia*, the European Atomic Energy Community (Euratom) was established, contains safeguards provisions that are similar to those of the Agency's Statute. These were elaborated in several regulations and the result was a system that is analogous to that of the Agency's Safeguards System of 1965. In the late 1950s the USA started transferring to Euratom the safeguards provided for in its bilateral agreements for cooperation with the various member states of the Community. The Agency's Board of Governors has never decided, however, that Euratom safeguards were "generally consistent" with those of the Agency and could be "accepted" by it. To make it nevertheless possible for nuclear material safeguarded by the Agency in a state outside Euratom to be transferred to a member of the Community, the practice was adopted of retransferring such material to the state originally supplying it, which would then transfer it to the intended recipient within Euratom. Once the agreement between the Community, its non-nuclear-weapon member states and the Agency enters into force, the question of general consistency between the two safeguards systems will lose its relevance.

group of the same type of facilities. For reactors and sealed stores this is 50 man-days, and for all other types of facilities the maximum inspection effort is made dependent on through-put of nuclear material, taking account of the strategic value of the amount and the nature of the material. For facilities involving plutonium or highly enriched uranium the maximum total of routine inspections per year is determined by multiplying the square root of the number of effective kilograms on inventory or annual through-put by 30. The minimum for such plants is 1.5 man-years.

The document further gives criteria for determining the intensity and duration, timing and mode of inspection; these include the form of nuclear material, its chemical composition, enrichment and accessibility, that is, generally, the "risk" associated with the material; the effectiveness of the state's accounting and control system; characteristics of the fuel cycle (whether, for example, there are plants in the state where the information obtained may be doublechecked or, conversely, which might help make the material more suitable for military use so that a higher effort is required, and so on). If the entire effort permitted for a given plant is not used up for that plant it may be applied, if necessary, at another facility of the same type in the state. If circumstances warrant, the Agency may make special inspections over and above the maximum.

In general, the inspection effort actually expended has so far remained well below the stipulated maximum. Although it may not have been the intention of the drafters of the "Blue Book" to give a quantification in addition to the *maxima* contained in that document, a number of states have insisted, in negotiating agreements, on being given in addition a clear indication of the actual inspection effort that would be made. The custom has therefore been established of including in each facility attachment of the Subsidiary Arrangements an indication of the actual routine inspection effort estimated to be made under ordinary circumstances, assuming that the circumstances at the facility remain as described in the design information provided and that the information on the national system also remains valid. Presumably, should the parameters on which the estimate is based change, a new figure will have to be agreed.

The rules on notice to be given before an inspection takes place are for INFCIRC/66/Rev.2 contained in the Inspectors Document [15 a]: for the NPT they are included in the agreements themselves. The basic rule in both is that one week's notice is to be given of routine inspections. INFCIRC/66/Rev.2 adds that whenever the Agency has the "right of access at all times", that is, when the facility contains or annually handles more than 60 kg of special fissionable material, no advance notice is required. INFCIRC/153 slightly refines this rule in saying, first, that only 24 hours notice need be given for visits to such "large" facilities and that, in addition, the Agency may carry out, without advance notification, a portion of its routine inspections.

The question of inspections without notice has been a moot point ever since the Agency began inspecting large facilities, for which this possibility was given. Objections have been raised to this procedure partly on practical grounds and partly as a matter of principle. The Statute [16], the Inspectors' Document [15 a] and the NPT-type agreements [1 r] all provide, on the one hand, that the state shall have the right to have its representatives accompany the inspectors during their inspections and, on the other, that the inspectors must not thereby be delayed or otherwise impeded in the exercise of their functions. Obviously, it is difficult in practice to arrange a meeting between inspector and escort if no notice is given of the pending arrival of the former, and certainly without his progress being delayed. None of the relevant documents contains a solution to this conundrum. The Safeguards System of 1965 simply provides that "actual procedures to implement these provisions shall be agreed upon between the parties concerned . . ."[8 b]. The "Blue Book" goes into a little more detail, in saying that whenever practicable and on the basis of the operational programme that is to be provided by the state, the Agency must from time to time give the state a general programme of announced and unannounced inspections. It adds that in carrying out unannounced inspections every effort should be made to minimize practical difficulties for facility operators and the state; particularly in respect of the state's right to have inspectors accompanied [1 g]. Again the practical solution is left to be thrashed out between the State and the Agency. Various measures have been tried, such as having the state nominate members of the facility staff as potential escorts, or having inspectors on their way to a facility pick up their escorts at an agreed location. But it has not always been possible so far to work out practical arrangements. For example, inspectors may arrive from abroad at a facility far from the state's capital, while the national authorities expect to have them escorted by someone normally stationed in the capital. In such cases it is quite possible that the inspectors are indeed delayed in the exercise of their functions. The question is whether the occasional delays that may occur are of really great technical importance——beyond causing temporary irritation——and whether it is not worth a short wait for the inspector to have someone with him who can help him gain smooth access to the strategic points he wishes to visit.

The principle involved is of a primarily technical nature: what is the purpose of a surprise inspection? Normally facilities are visited routinely at more or less regular intervals, to check receipts or shipments, and once or several times a year to verify the physical inventory taking. There may be some facilities, containing highly enriched uranium or plutonium in readily accessible form, such as large fast critical assemblies, where it would be possible to divert material between inspection visits. It would be a great coincidence if an inspector should catch an operator in the process of diverting a small part of his material. The "cops and robbers" approach of making frequent spot checks to detect diversion or at least deter it through the risk of being caught red-handed, if it was ever applied by the Agency, has certainly now been abandoned. In most cases, therefore, there should be little objection to giving advance notice of inspections. To cover all eventualities, however——for example to make certain, by a surprise visit, that no reprocessing work is actually done during the supposed clean-out period of a reprocessing plant——the Agency should have the right to make unannounced inspections even if it makes sporadic use of it.

Sooner or later the inspection workload in a given state or region, combined with the presence of installations that require continuous inspection (year round or for limited periods), may make it desirable to establish resident inspection offices outside Agency headquarters. This will, of course, necessitate the elaboration of detailed arrangements with the state or states concerned. These arrangements will have to cover, among other things, the question of notice of inspections, which will then involve a completely new set of practical problems.

The last differences between the two documents to be discussed are the rules for exemption and other provisions to set aside the application of certain safeguards measures. First, exemptions. INFCIRC/66/Rev.2 permits the exemption——on request of the state——of up to one kilogram of plutonium, and its quantitative equivalent in each of the other categories of nuclear material: enriched, natural and depleted uranium, and thorium. These totals——which may not be exceeded at any time——are applicable to the state as a whole [8 c]. Further, the document provides for the exemption of plutonium generated in reactors that produce no more than 100 g of this element annually and reactors of very low power. Thus, the plutonium in many research reactors is disregarded [8 d].

INFCIRC/153 has a quantitative exemption rule [1 h] exactly like the one in the earlier document. In addition, it allows exemption without any upper limit of particular nuclear materials, or materials used for specific purposes, that is, nuclear material "used in gram quantities or less" as a sensing component in measuring instruments——for example, plutonium-beryllium sources. It also exempts nuclear material used in non-nuclear activities which may subsequently be recovered and used again in nuclear activities——such as depleted uranium used for shielding purposes, and plutonium containing 80 per cent or more PU-238 (which is hard to handle in any great quantity, because of its high temperature and radioactivity) used as the source of energy in pacemakers for heart patients [1 i]. The "reactor exemption" described above has remained peculiar to INFCIRC/66/Rev.2.

The quantitative exemptions have been included in the two documents to allow small quantities of nuclear material to be disregarded for the purposes of reporting and verification, particularly when they are used in facilities outside nuclear research centres, such as hospitals or universities, that may wish to avoid maintaining an accounting apparatus merely for the sake of such minor amounts. As often as not, however, using the exemption possibility is more trouble than it is worth: most states have internal requirements for careful bookkeeping on the most minute quantities of nuclear material, and the administrative bother involved in obtaining exemption and keeping track of the national total to ensure that this is not exceeded may lead to much additional accounting. In practice, under INFCIRC/ 153, it may be easier to deal with most small quantities together in one material balance area composed of "locations of nuclear material outside facilities" [1 j], with minimal reporting requirements.

Under INFCIRC/66/Rev.2 the application of safeguards may be temporarily set aside by means of suspension. This may be applied when nuclear material in quantities below the exemption limits just discussed is transferred to another facility, where no safeguards are applied, within the state or outside it, for reprocessing, fabrication or testing. Suspension of safeguards with respect to nuclear material may also take place when equivalent amounts of similar material that were not previously safeguarded have been substituted therefor [8 e]. Clearly, neither case will arise under an NPT-type agreement where all nuclear material in all peaceful activities in the state is under safeguards and with safeguards following on export. INFCIRC/153, therefore, has no suspension provisions.

It contains a more cogent system of termination, however, than does

4

INFCIRC/66/Rev.2. As discussed before[11] this document gives conditions for termination upon export which, in NPT situations, arise partly from that treaty. In addition, under the older document, termination takes place with respect to nuclear material which was subject to safeguards (because it was used in a facility that had been supplied under or submitted to safeguards) when that material is no longer in that facility and does not contain any safeguarded plutonium [8 f]. Furthermore, safeguards are terminated when the Agency has determined that the material has been consumed or so diluted that it is no longer usable for any nuclear activity relevant from the point of safeguards, or has become "practicably irrecoverable" [8 g].

INFCIRC/153 contains the same provision on consumption and dilution [1 k], but it goes further. It says that where the conditions of that provision are not met, for example, when material is not practicably irrecoverable, but the state considers (for economic reasons, for instance) that the recovery of material from residues is not for the time being practicable or desirable, there must be consultation on the safeguards measures to be applied [1 l]. If material is to be used in non-nuclear activities (the examples cited are the production of alloys or ceramics) the state and the Agency must agree on the circumstances under which safeguards may be terminated [1 m]; they must in any case be terminated if it is agreed that the material is practicably irrecoverable as a result of the non-nuclear use [1 l]. Wherever possible, for instance when a particular facility has the established practice of shipping out nuclear material for non-nuclear purposes, the necessary "agreement" between the state and the Agency is laid down in the relevant facility attachment, thus obviating consultation each time such a shipment is to be made.

The distinction in the undertakings around which the two documents are constructed leads to one very basic difference in the provisions on non-application. INFCIRC/66/Rev.2 is meant to be used in connection with "safeguards agreements", which are defined as agreements which contain an undertaking "not to use certain items in such a way as to further any military purpose . . ." [8 h]. INFCIRC/153, giving effect to Article III.1 of the NPT, accordingly has "the exclusive purpose" of verifying that states party to the treaty do not "divert nuclear energy from peaceful uses to nuclear weapons or other nuclear explosive devices". It does not seek to interfere with military, non-explosive uses of nuclear material, such as, for instance, the propulsion of naval ships by means of a nuclear reactor.

This has led to a problem, because the use of nuclear material for military purposes is by definition cloaked in secrecy and closed to international safeguards. Understanding this, the drafters of the "Blue Book" nevertheless did not wish the non-explosive, military use to become a gap in the system, through which material could be easily diverted to the manufacture of explosive devices. They therefore worked out a scheme [1 n] that would leave as small as possible an interval between the moment when the nuclear material would be withdrawn from the safeguards regime and the time when it would come back. They provided that parties should make special arrangements identifying, as far as possible, the period or circumstances of the non-application, and laid upon the state the task of informing the

---

[11] See pp. 37–38.

Agency of the total quantity and composition of the nuclear material. On the other hand, they provided that the arrangement should only be on the time of use of the material and on procedures, reporting and so on, and would not involve any "approval or classified knowledge of the military activity or relate to the use of the nuclear material therein". Perhaps there is a contradiction inherent in these two provisions, but this remains to be seen. So far, the article has not been applied, and it must be remembered that application is only possible if a state has nuclear material in respect of which it had not given a promise that it should be used only for non-military purposes, and to which Agency safeguards applied under another agreement. For example, no nuclear material may be used for a military purpose that is supplied by the USA under a bilateral cooperation agreement on which the safeguards were transferred to the IAEA.

V. *Recruitment and designation of inspectors*

Article XII.B of the Statute empowers the Agency to "establish a staff of inspectors". Neither the Statute nor INFCIRC/66/Rev.2 expressly says that these should be staff members of the Agency. In 1961, however, the Board of Governors decided that the inspector general and all officers of professional grade of (what was then) the Division of Inspection would be appointed by the director general as "staff officials" of the Agency [17]. INFCIRC/153 uses the term "Agency official" [1 o]. To make sure that inspectors are subject to the Agency's rules pertaining to their conduct, it is of course essential that they should be staff members.

In principle, inspectors are recruited like any other Agency staff member, the "paramount consideration" being "to secure employees of the highest standards of efficiency, technical competence, and integrity" [16 b]. The second consideration is that "due regard shall be paid to the contributions of members to the Agency and to the importance of recruiting the staff on as wide a geographical basis as possible" [16 b]. This means that, as in other organizations of the United Nations family, there are quotas for each member state—based usually on its financial contributions to the budget—but also that every effort should be made to recruit from as many states as possible. In practice, the distribution of nationalities within the Agency's Department of Safeguards and Inspection differs somewhat from that of the Agency as a whole. This has several reasons. First, the number of disciplines from which the safeguards inspectors may be recruited tends to be limited. Second, the developed nations are often in a better position to provide staff with the required qualifications than are other states. Third, two factors must be taken into account in recruiting inspectors: (1) that some states wish to admit as inspectors only citizens from countries that have accepted safeguards, and (2) that one cannot arbitrarily send all nationals everywhere. In the sensitive area of international inspection it is important that visits to a given country are made only by citizens of states with which that country maintains good relations. Nevertheless there is a wide distribution of nationalities in the department; the present total of 59 inspectors comes from 36 states—the USA, USSR, UK, Italy and the Federal Republic of Germany being the best represented, in that order.

So far, all inspectors have been recruited at the professional level; most of them are physical or chemical engineers; some are mathematicians, statisticians or accountants. If the Agency's safeguards activities should increase greatly, the recruitment of technicians rather than professionals may have to be considered. So far, there has not been an occasion to do so. Some governments have already stated their preference for professional level inspectors; also, facility operators generally prefer that the staff carrying out inspections possess the same technical competence as the plant staff with whom they deal, who are usually of fairly senior status.

Recruitment is not always easy, particularly for the lower professional ranks. In addition to having an adequate professional and academic background, inspectors should possess a great deal of tact, be adaptable to difficult situations, be willing to travel for long periods to remote and not always attractive locations (nuclear plants tend to be constructed outside urban areas); they should preferably speak several languages and they should be willing to do a job which may keep them away for a long time from their purely technical or research interests, although those who have the knack can contribute much by working out procedures and helping to develop instruments. It remains to be seen what the long-run career prospects will be for young men entering the Agency as safeguards inspectors. Most inspectors function at headquarters as "country officers" or "facility officers"; they deal with safeguards for a particular state or facility, handle the necessary correspondence and maintain appropriate contact with officials from these states. Not every technical man is inclined towards this kind of semi-administrative paper work. Those who are, and who are at present employed by the Agency, constitute a highly competent cadre of specialists in a very complicated and difficult subject.

New staff members do not start off making inspections in the field right away. They first undergo several months' on-the-job training at headquarters, familiarizing themselves with the main documents, safeguards procedures, codified practices and the operation of such safeguards devices as surveillance cameras, measurement instruments for non-destructive assay of nuclear material, and seals. Lately, formalized training courses lasting several weeks have been held. The Agency intends to extend this training to include refresher courses to acquaint staff who have already been employed for a while with the latest safeguards methods and techniques.

Once a new recruit has joined the Department of Safeguards and Inspection the director general seeks the approval of the Board of Governors to use him as a safeguards inspector. This is done both for officials joining the Department's Division of Operations—whose main job it is to perform inspections—and for staff of the Division of Development—who will participate only sporadically in inspections to make their specialized knowledge available in complicated verification operations, to help out where extra staff is needed, or to try out new methods and techniques for development purposes. Before formally advising the Board of the names and nationalities of the staff he wishes to use as inspectors, the director general also gives the Board members confidential summaries of each person's relevant qualifications. The Board thus has the opportunity to judge both these qualifications and the geographic composition of the Agency's safeguards inspectorate [17].

There is relatively little turnover in the operational staff. Most staff members in the Division of Operations are given an initial two-year contract which, when satisfactorily completed, is followed by a series of five-year appointments. The policy that inspectors should be long-term staff members over whom the Agency will have a maximum disciplinary authority is in line with the wishes of most of the states involved.

Once an official is approved to be used as an inspector, and is trained, the designation process is put into motion for the state or states where he is expected to function. The various stages in the designation procedure are described in the Inspectors Document which applies to the inspectors who work under the Safeguards System of 1965 [15 c]. This is as three-step procedure: first, a letter is sent to the state, giving the name, nationality and grade of the inspector proposed, together with written certification of his relevant qualifications. The state is expected to accept or reject the proposed designation within 30 days. If accepted, the inspector is designated and the state accordingly informed. If the state rejects the proposal, the Agency should propose an alternative. Over the years it has become customary to add another step, that is, informal consultations with officials of the government regarding the acceptability of the persons concerned, before the letter containing the formal proposal is sent. For the sake of simplification and in order to gain time, this preliminary consultation has now been omitted except when governments have clearly stated a preference for continuing it, or when there are political considerations that make prior informal consultation desirable.

The "Blue Book" [1 p] contains essentially the same provisions as the Inspectors Document except that it leaves no doubt that only staff members of the Agency can be safeguards inspectors [1 p]: the rule is added that either upon the request of the state or on his own initiative the director general shall inform the state of the withdrawal of any inspector for that state.

Both documents provide that a state's repeated refusal to accept the designation of Agency inspectors may be brought to the Board of Governors for appropriate action, if the director general believes that such a refusal would impede the Agency's inspections. Theoretically, a state might reject proposals for nomination until, by elimination, only the inspectors whom it preferred would be left. Presumably the Board of Governors would object to such selective practices. It may also be assumed that an objection would have to be voiced if the state, by repeated rejections, should unduly delay the start of inspection. Such a deliberate delay might be seen as non-compliance with its obligation to cooperate with the Agency for the administration of safeguards, as is required by the agreements concluded under the Safeguards System of 1965; this rule is also contained in INFCIRC/153 [1 q]. This latter document stipulates further that the Board of Governors may take recourse to the sanctions provided for in the Statute if it finds that the Agency is not able to verify that no diversion has taken place. This situation could in theory arise if——through the repeated refusal of the state to accept inspectors——no inspections could be made. It may be noted here that the "Blue Book" also provides that when a new NPT-type agreement enters into force, and the Agency therefore needs inspectors to verify design information and the information contained in the initial reports on nuclear material, the designation procedures should be completed, if possible, within 30 days after the entry into force. If this cannot be done, inspectors should be temporarily designated.

It has never been necessary for the director general to bring any violation of these provisions before the Board. In general, the designation procedure seems to work quite smoothly, except that on a few occasions states have objected to what they considered to be an overly large number of proposed designations. Many governments appear to prefer to keep the number of inspectors designated for their state as low as possible. The Agency, on the other hand, has an interest in having enough inspectors for each state to allow some flexibility in the planning of inspection trips. Other pressing work, holidays or sickness may prevent inspectors from being available, and yet the Agency needs enough expert staff to deal with the various facilities to be covered during any given inspection. Moreover, it is desirable for an inspector to be designated for more than one state in a region; he may then inspect facilities in several states on one trip, thereby saving travel funds. Usually only a part of the inspectors designated for a given state would participate at the same time in an inspection there, so that as a rule the number of inspectors simultaneously present at a single installation would be smaller than the total number designated for the country.

References

1. INFCIRC/153.
   (a) ---, paragraph 39.
   (b) --, paragraph 94.
   (c) --, paragraph 34(a).
   (d) --, paragraph 7.
   (e) ---, paragraph 31.
   (f) --, paragraph 32.
   (g) --, paragraph 84.
   (h) --, paragraph 37.
   (i) --, paragraph 36.
   (j) --, paragraphs 106 and 110.
   (k) --, paragraph 11.
   (l) --, paragraph 35.
   (m) --, paragraph 13.
   (n) --, paragraph 14.
   (o) --, paragraph 85(a).
   (p) --, paragraphs 9 and 85.
   (q) --, paragraph 3.
   (r) --, paragraph 89.
2. INFCIRC/5, II (paragraph 4) and III Article V(a).
3. INFCIRC/36.
4. INFCIRC/57.
5. INFCIRC/86.
6. INFCIRC/171.
7. Eighteen Nation Committee on Disarmament (ENDC).
   (a) --, ENDC/207.
   (b) --, ENDC/206.
8. INFCIRC/66/Rev. 2.
   (a) --, paragraphs 26(a), 28(a) and 74(a).
   (b) --, paragraph 50.
   (c) --, paragraph 21.
   (d) --, paragraph 22.

    (e) ––, paragraphs 24 and 25.
    (f) ––, paragraph 26(b).
    (g) ––, paragraph 26(c).
    (h) ––, paragraph 82. See also above p. 10.
9. See, for instance, the statements by the delegates of Japan and the Netherlands, reported in GC(IX)/OR.94, paragraphs 10 and 112.
10. INFCIRC/207.
11. See also Willrich, M. and Taylor, Th.B., *Nuclear Theft: Risks and Safeguards*, a report to the Energy Policy Project of the Ford Foundation (Cambridge, Mass., Ballinger Publishing Co., 1974).
12. Scheinman, L., "Safeguarding nuclear materials". in *Science and Public Affairs,* Vol. XXX, No. 4, July 1974.
13. Various proposals for measures by governments, alone or in conjunction, which might decrease physical security risks involving nuclear material are made by Prawitz, J., "Arguments for extended NPT safeguards", in *Nuclear Proliferation Problems* (Stockholm, Almqvist & Wiksell, Stockholm International Peace Research Institute; Cambridge, Mass. and London, the MIT Press) pp. 162–63.
14. Rainer, R. and Sanders, B., "The IAEA NPT Safeguards––National Control and International Safeguards", in *Nuclear Proliferation Problems* (see reference [13] above).
    (a) ––, p. 135 *et seq.*
    (b) ––, p. 140.
15. General Conference Document.
    (a) ––, GC(V)/INF/39, Annex.
    (b) ––, Annex paragraph 5.
    (c) ––, Annex, paragraphs 1 and 2.
16. IAEA Statue
    (a) ––, Article XII.A.6.
    (b) ––, Article VII.D.
17. Szasz, Paul C.,"The Law and Practices of the International Atomic Energy Agency", IAEA Legal Series No. 7, Vienna, 1970, paragraph 21.8.1.1.

4. Funds and figures

I. *Financing safeguards*

Ever since the inception of Agency safeguards it had been the practice that the costs of implementation were covered under the administrative expenses in the annual budget. The contributions to this budget were based on the United Nations scale of assessments.

When the Agency's safeguards operations began to reach sizeable proportions, some member states voiced doubt that this approach was appropriate. They referred to the Statute [1] which makes it possible in principle for the Board of Governors to deduct "such amounts as are recoverable under agreements regarding the application of safeguards . . .", a possibility of which no use had been made. In 1964 the Board of Governors discussed the question who should pay for safeguards, but it deferred consideration until further additional experience had been gained. The matter was discussed virtually every year thereafter, but no definite progress was made towards settling the issue until 1970. The question had come up again in 1969, during the discussions on the budget estimates for 1970, and it was then recommended that a study group should be set up to examine it. Because by the time the 1970 Safeguards Committee met the matter had still not been finalized, the Board decided in June 1970 to expand the terms of reference of the committee by requesting that it also discuss the problem of safeguards finances.

When discussions began, there was a wide gap between the opinions of two participating groups. One of these, consisting mainly of developing nations, reasoned that identifiable costs of the application of safeguards should be reimbursed by the states concerned, and that Article XIV C of the Statute should be applied for this purpose. They expressed particular concern that the financing of safeguards would eventually place a heavy burden on developing countries having little or no nuclear activity. They called on the nuclear-weapon states to bear a percentage of the total safeguards costs that should not be less than their percentage contribution under the United Nations scale of assessments; the remaining proportion of safeguards costs should be shared by non-nuclear-weapon states on the basis of the volume of safeguards work actually performed by the Agency in each such state. Some added that the application of safeguards under the United Kingdom and the United States offers should be paid for entirely by those two states.[1]. They agreed, however, that costs of research and development in respect of safeguards should be funded in the same way as other Agency activities.

The other group of participating governments emphasized that safeguards, and particularly those applied under the NPT, were in the interest of all members of the world community. The states with the lowest rates of assessment would, in any case, pay relatively little. As one of the statutory activities of the Agency, safeguards should be funded from the regular budget, they said, as had been the case hitherto.

---

[1] See p. 29.

The two groups submitted formal proposals expressing their different views. After long debate a compromise was reached. It provided that the costs the Agency would incur in applying safeguards in member states would continue to be met from the regular budget, but that the method of assessing members for contributions would be adjusted so as to limit the share of these costs borne by members having low *per capita* net national products. This solution was endorsed by the Board on 20 April 1971, approved by the General Conference in September of that year and applied in fixing the scale of assessment for members contributing towards the IAEA's administrative expenses for the budgets beginning in 1972.

One of the results of this arrangement is that all countries falling under this rule have paid the same amount towards safeguards in 1972 and 1973 as they paid in 1971, and that they will again pay the same for 1975 and 1976. The states that made the lowest contribution to the regular budget (of which in 1974 there were 28) have for each of the years 1971-73 contributed $754 each for safeguards. For the contribution to safeguards for 1974 the latter states were assessed at $841. Because the base rates of assessment of these countries for their contribution to the regular budget in 1975 were reduced to 0.02 per cent, in accordance with the principles adopted by the United Nations General Assembly and applied in the UN scale for 1974-76, their assessment for costs is again the minimum, that is, $754. In the scale of assessment for 1974, the 71 member states having low *per capita*, national products were required to contribute a total of $280 686 (6.67664 per cent) towards the total safeguards estimate of $4 204 000, while the remaining $3 923 314 (93.32336 per cent) was called for from the 31 other member states included in the scale. The detailed arrangements are set out in Annex 2. It will be noted that they were adopted on the understanding that they were to be reviewed at an appropriate time after 1975.

From these figures it will be seen that the cost of safeguards, especially to the Agency's less well-endowed member states, cannot be considered a financial burden of consequence.

II. *Statistics*

As of 31 December 1974 the status of signatures and ratifications of, or accessions to, the NPT and of the conclusion of the necessary agreements with the Agency was as follows:

Number of non-nuclear-weapon states that had signed the NPT   95
Number of non-nuclear-weapon states that have become party
   of the NPT through ratification or accession[2]   80
Number of non-nuclear-weapon states party to the NPT with   35
   which safeguards agreements in connection with the
   treaty were in force

In addition by the date, 12 non-nuclear-weapon states party to the NPT had negotiated the required safeguards agreements with the Agency, that is, these

[2] States that accede to the Treaty are not among those which have previously signed it.

agreements had been approved by the Agency's Board of Governors and were awaiting entry into force. The total of 47 includes 22, that is, almost all, non-nuclear-weapon states party to the NPT that have significant nuclear activities. All but one of the remaining 25 states that had negotiated such agreements have neither nuclear material exceeding the quantitative exemption limitations given in the agreement nor nuclear material in a facility; in concluding the agreement they also concluded a protocol deferring the application of safeguards until they would have a quantity of nuclear material exceeding those limits.

Among the NPT states which had concluded a safeguards agreement with the Agency there are 10 that are also parties to the Treaty for the Prohibition of Nuclear Weapons in Latin America (the Treaty of Tlatelolco); two of these agreements were in force; the rest were awaiting entry into force. Such agreements as a rule contain a preamble referring to both treaties. Alternatively, a special protocol is concluded referring to the Treaty of Tlatelolco. In one case, Panama, the text contained in INFCIRC/153 has been used as the basis for an agreement with a state that is a party to the Treaty of Tlatelolco only.

In March 1970, when the NPT entered into force, the IAEA was applying safeguards in 32 states, under 44 safeguards agreements concluded either under the Safeguards System of 1965 or the system preceding this. As of 31 December 1974, 59 such safeguards agreements had been concluded, now involving 34 states. For 12 of these states, which had meanwhile become parties to the NPT and concluded the appropriate safeguards agreements with the Agency, the application of safeguards under earlier agreements is suspended. It is worth noting, however, that since the entry into force of the NPT the total number of agreements concluded under the Safeguards System of 1965 has increased. Since, by definition, such agreements are concluded only with states that have significant nuclear activities, one may conclude that the number of agreements under document INFCIRC/66/Rev.2 is still increasing faster than those entered into under document INFCIRC/153 with states that have nuclear activities warranting application of safeguards. The application of Article III.2 will probably contribute further to this increase, but, in noting this, one should remenber that agreements concluded under the former safeguards document may be of narrower coverage than NPT-type agreements.

In respect of the safeguards agreements under INFCIRC/66/Rev.2 the Agency takes action only upon the request of the state or states concerned. In regard to agreements in connection with the NPT, however, the Agency follows a more active policy. Although neither a party to the treaty nor appointed to function as its administrative arm, the Agency helps states to conclude the necessary safeguards agreements, by maintaining during its annual General Conferences an office where interested delegates can, if they wish, enter into negotiations, and by keeping contact on the subject through the IAEA offices in New York and Geneva, through UNDP resident representatives in the field and in some cases by direct correspondence with states involved.

It is fair to say that as soon as all agreements now approved by the Agency's Board of Governors enter into force, Agency safeguards, by virtue of the NPT or otherwise, will cover by far the greater part of the peaceful nuclear activities of the non-nuclear-weapon states. Exceptions include Egypt, which has a research reactor that is not under international safeguards; India and Israel, where safeguards are applied to only part of the nuclear installations in operation; and South Africa, where the isotope enrichment pilot plant, as far as is known from published reports, is either under construction or already operating. Moreover, although in some countries Agency safeguards under the Safeguards System of 1965 actually cover all peaceful nuclear activities, there is nothing to prohibit those countries from starting other, non-safeguarded nuclear activities, either with their own efforts and material, or with the assistance of states that do not insist that international safeguards be applied in respect of the items they sell or the nuclear material used or produced by means of them.

Reference

1. IAEA Statute, Article XIV C.

5. Further developments

I. *The next steps*

It is fair to say that both safeguards documents and the agreements that are based on them generally give the Agency the legal tools to achieve its objectives. Any flaws that might be found in the application of safeguards would be due to the way in which the documents are implemented rather than to any inherent inadequacy in them; even document INFCIRC/66/Rev.2, with all its shortcomings, leaves enough flexibility to permit reasonable application. INFCIRC/153 — an extremely careful compromise between technical needs and political possibilities — is more explicit in its provisions and may make it easier to avoid misunderstandings and frictions with national authorities to which the potentially more indiscriminate application permitted by INFCIRC/66/Rev.2 might lead. The limitations INFCIRC/153 imposes on the Agency are stricter, particularly in respect of inspection effort and access. It is not yet possible to say whether these limitations are perhaps too restrictive; the Agency has not yet had to deal under an NPT type agreement with any facility handling so much nuclear material of high strategic value that it might have exhausted its maximum permissible effort. One may expect that when that times comes, techniques and instruments will have been developed which can adequately supplement the inspection effort.

The prospects are that, for the foreseeable future, both documents will have to be applied. If so, there is a case for improving and updating INFCIRC/66/Rev. 2 so that it becomes a self-contained document along the lines of INFCIRC/153. There are indications that one reason why some developed industrial nations are slow to accept the NPT is that they have concluded that they can continue to receive nuclear supplies also under the INFCIRC/66/Rev. 2 safeguards regime. One gets the impression, for example, that for the supply by the United States of nuclear facilities and materials, the safeguards involved may be based on the traditional type of agreement rather than on the NPT type [1]. The same appears to apply with respect to some other important supplier states. Whether this represents a change of policy among the depository powers of the NPT remains to be seen. Hitherto it seemed to have been their policy to give preferential treatment to parties to the treaty [2]; those who had joined the NPT would be "rewarded" by being able to conclude an "easier" and more up-to-date INFCIRC/153 agreement, whereas those who did not would be "punished" by being supplied only under INFCIRC/66/Rev. 2 conditions. As an incentive for adherence to the NPT, this has not worked. The reasons vary, but it is clear that as long as states find that they can go on receiving nuclear supplies, even from NPT parties, under INFCIRC/66/Rev. 2 safeguards that are connected only with such supplies, they may prefer not to submit to safeguards on all their peaceful nuclear activities, under INFCIRC/153. Obviously the Agency must face the fact that it will have to continue applying safeguards also outside the framework of the treaty.

One conclusion is that the time may have come to review and update INFCIRC/66/Rev. 2. The possibility of giving a more precise definition of the technical scope and procedures of that document, to make it reflect the considerable development in accounting concepts, statistical methods and surveillance and containment techniques that has occurred in the six years since it was last extended, was mentioned by the director general at the last General Conference. He was supported by several speakers, notably the delegate of the USSR. An alternative would be to apply INFCIRC/153 agreements to non-NPT circumstances, but this will not always be possible; under the Safeguards System of 1965 part of the peaceful nuclear fuel cycle may be covered, whereas INFCIRC/153 is based on the assumption that the entire peaceful nuclear effort is submitted to safeguards. It is therefore likely that moves will soon be made to update INFCIRC/66/Rev.2.

In this context the provision should be remembered [3] that the "principles and procedures set forth in this document shall be subject to periodic review in the light of the further experience gained by the Agency as well as of technological developments". Annexes I and II to INFCIRC/66/Rev. 2 (which constitute the reviews made of this document, in 1966 and 1968, respectively) are expressly called "provisional" and provide that "they shall be subject to review at any time and shall in any case be reviewed after two years experience of their application has been gained".

In the short term, the application of safeguards under INFCIRC/66/Rev. 2 could perhaps to some extent be brought up-to-date by a closer adaptation of the Subsidiary Arrangements to the type used under INFCIRC/153. This could only be a temporary solution, however.

An important argument for adapting and modernizing the Safeguards System of 1965 is the need for standardization of the agreements concluded outside the framework of the NPT. This would help to avoid the at present quite considerable differences between the terms of some of those agreements, and it would facilitate the application of safeguards. If it were, in fact, possible to proceed along the lines of INFCIRC/153 and achieve what amounts to a combination of safeguards system and standard agreement, this would make it much easier to negotiate such agreements and would also bring about the necessary degree of standardization. But before this point is reached there is a great deal of work to be done.

II. *Safeguards Research and Development (R&D)*

To some extent the whole field of nuclear safeguards is still open to experiment and development. Operational experience is still being written down. Safeguards practices are continually improved. Methods are adapted to new requirements and simplified wherever possible, and results are evaluated in the light of the effort spent, to reach optimum effectiveness relative to cost. Initially, the Agency's Department of Safeguards and Inspection contained a single division which was charged with both application and development. By late 1968, however, the operational responsibilities had become so large and there was so much developmental work to be done that it became necessary to establish a separate division for this purpose. Although the main task of the Division of Development is research and development, it is frequently associated with operational work when new tasks are to be performed in the field or when the complexity of operations requires specialized support. The Division of Operations, in its turn, contributes to development; it helps to work out new procedures and techniques, prepares manuals on inspection practices, formulates its needs for new instruments, assists in their development and tests them *in situ*. The exchange of views between the two units is continuous and productive. Description of the development in progress is therefore not just a summing up of jobs done by the Division of Development; neither are the references to the application of safeguards elsewhere in this paper exclusively related to the activities of the Division of Operations. Both divisions are engaged in formulating conceptual approaches, and although for any given task the emphasis may be in one or another organizational unit, the resulting policies are as a rule generated by the Department as a whole.

The developmental work of the Agency in the field of safeguards may, for convenience, be divided into three general categories; the dividing lines between these are not sharply drawn and there is inevitably some overlap between them. The categories comprise: (*a*) the conceptual formulation of problems, the general approach to their solution and the requirements that must be met to obtain such solutions; (*b*) the development of methods and techniques and of the devices necessary to apply such techniques, and (*c*) the testing of procedures and devices under operating conditions and the codification of procedures on the basis of such tests.

The first category involves the systems analysis activities that lead to the optimization of the results of the Agency's safeguards as against their cost. It includes the defining of safeguards requirements for various types of facilities, the elaboration of procedures to evaluate the accuracy of accounting and effectiveness of safeguards, studies on the quantification of results, and the elaboration of methods for the electronic processing of data so as (*a*) to make the best possible use of the information received by the Agency, and (*b*) to simplify safeguards operations. Much of this work is done with the help of groups of experts from a number of states with particular experience in the specific field to be covered. Thus, the conceptual approaches elaborated by the Agency comprise the input of philosophy and experience from many different quarters, which not only enhances their quality but also their acceptability.

The development of methods and techniques has the twofold purpose of obtaining *modus operandi* and instrumentation that will yield the most meaningful information, while making safeguards as unintrusive as possible. The work comprises the elaboration of procedures, the development of various instruments and techniques, particularly for non-destructive measurements, devising tamper-proof or tamper-indicating devices for unattended surveillance of safe-guarded facilities and instruments to monitor the flow of nuclear material in various kinds of plants. Most of the work in this field is done under contract outside the Agency by a large number of research institutes in member states. The IAEA's financial contributions to this work are relatively small. In 1972 it paid about $200 000; in 1973 $160 000. It is expected that in 1974 the contribution will be even less, although in 1975 it is likely to rise to about $300 000. Thus, at relatively little cost, the Agency obtains a high yield in terms of methods and techniques. It also functions usefully as a coordinator of and a channel for the exchange of information on the developmental work under way, planned or needed in the area of safeguards.

The testing of techniques and methods and the codification of the resulting procedures is a very important part of the developmental work. Here, again, the IAEA relies heavily on the active support of its member states, which lend their facilities for this purpose and make experts available to help prepare procedures. The "Grey Book" is one of the results of this international cooperation.

In discussions of safeguards—particularly among non-technicians—wistful mention has often been made of the need for "black boxes" that would produce all necessary information and largely obviate the need for human intrusion during inspections. The development work done, sponsored, and coordinated by the Agency has not so far been able to produce this kind of magic.[1] It takes time to progress from the idea to the point where, for instance a workable instrument—trustworthy, tamper-resistant, preferably portable and not too expensive—can be certified for operational use. But the development efforts have already contributed much in improving safeguards techniques, yielding more significant data while reducing the intrusiveness of inspection. Much work remains to be done.

III. *Conclusions*

Safeguards have by now successfully outgrown the experimental stage. If safeguards help to delay and prevent proliferation of nuclear weapons, or at least contribute to the confidence that a given state is not using its peaceful nuclear activities for military purposes, they will have justified their existence. They also constitute a unique exercise in international verification, which may eventually set a useful precedent for "real" disarmament measures, if not applicable in their entirety then in part: as an example, perhaps, of an international arrangement to gather data on the production of certain materials and devices, and of the manner in which use can be made of national systems of accounting and control.

It is sometimes argued that once new techniques, such as laser beams, become practical in the detonation of hydrogen weapons, safeguards against the diversion of nuclear material will have outlived their usefulness. This is like saying that since it is possible to purchase howitzers there is no further need to license and control handguns. There will be an ever increasing amount of special fissionable materials in circulation, and these will have to be controlled nationally and internationally. The fact that there may be other more efficient means of mass destruction does not make fission bombs any less dangerous.

---

[1] Much development work has been devoted to methods for safeguarding isotopic enrichment plants. Account has been taken in this context of the possible wish of the states concerned to set up—in terms of INFCIRC/153, paragraph 46(b) (iv)—"a special material balance area around a process step involving commercially sensitive information". This approach may be inversely compared to that of the "black box" in its usual connotations; in this case, rather than the Agency having exclusive access to a closed device that would yield it all the data needed to apply safeguards, the operator has the exclusive access to a given area and the Agency must find its significant information elsewhere.

Safeguards keep pace with the growth of the nuclear industry. Under conditions of present growth, the techniques and the manpower resources now available are adequate for the time being. Over the longer term there are several potential factors which may make it easier for safeguards to keep up with the increased use of nuclear materials: (1) as more countries acquire complete nuclear fuel cycles. the emphasis on strategically important stages in the cycle will mean a relative simplification of the safeguards effort; (2) as more governments establish sophisticated systems of accounting for and control of nuclear material, the safeguarding organizations will be able to make better use of the information provided; and (3), as experience grows and development leads to better results, improved techniques and more effective instruments can be applied. There may be some validity in the objection that, with the growth of the nuclear industry, a "confidence level" of 95 per cent or more may still leave a considerable gap and large quantities of material not accounted for. But there is reason to expect that this gap will narrow with improved measurement techniques and more effective measures for physical security. In any case, there would seem to be no alternative. One may reason that *no safeguards* would be preferable to *inadequate safeguards*, because the latter might create a false impression of security. This is true. But, a control that yields a confidence level of somewhat less than 100 per cent is better than no control, as long as one remains aware of the shortcomings of the system.

Will the growing nuclear industry continue to tolerate the application of safeguards? In practice, the "burden" is much less heavy than originally feared. Safeguards are in any case a minor price to pay, given the inherent dangers of the processes and the materials used. National governments will continue to keep an extremely careful eye on the nuclear industry, against which the additional intrusion by an international body could be easily discounted.

In the long term, the IAEA will be concerned with a number of practical problems. Competent staff must be attracted, who will remain engaged in a responsible, difficult and in the long run possibly somewhat boring task. The organization and the states concerned must somehow be assured of the lasting vigilance and incorruptibility of the staff. The administrative problems will increase in complexity, but they are not insoluble.

One may ask whether an international organization, like the IAEA, has the operational and administrative apparatus to continue functioning effectively, in the face of the political and bureaucratic encumbrances that beset so many such bodies. At present––partly, perhaps, because the safeguards operation is still imbued with much youthful enthusiasm––the apparatus, although somewhat cumbersome, seems to work. There are factors, including political ones, that may have an adverse effect on efficiency. The Agency must try to subsist at the highest possible level of technical competence, in a political environment; it must take account of politics while avoiding becoming too political.

At various times since the inception of the Agency's safeguards task, some persons have advocated separating this undertaking from the remainder of the Agency's activities, so that the promotional––and, particularly, technical assist-ance––activities would not suffer from an emphasis on the regulatory work of safeguards. To some degree this dichotomy is already reflected in the IAEA's budget practices. But it is the opinion of this writer that such an organizational split-off would be a dangerous move that would benefit neither the Agency as a whole, nor safeguards. Nuclear energy, after all, has both a beneficial and a dangerous side. It is only natural that these two aspects should be reflected in one organization which promotes the benefits and tries to prevent the dangers. The two tasks are logically inseparable. The imposition of restraints should go apace with the increase of the peaceful applications. The two sides should be balanced, and the Agency is in a position to do this.

Practically, also, the two categories of activity should rely on a single administrative apparatus. Furthermore, safeguards itself have a promotional side; the IAEA is in a good position to advise on the establishment of national systems for accountancy and control and on measures for physical protection. And, finally: safeguards are not only a restraint on certain actions; by reducing the dangers, they should be a factor in the promotion of the peaceful use of nuclear energy.

An essential conclusion to be drawn from the experience gained so far with Agency safeguards—using the term "safeguards" to cover a range of activities, from the negotiation of the underlying agreement to the verification of a physical inventory in a facility at the end of a material balance period—is that the effectiveness of the entire exercise depends on the cooperation of the state concerned and each of the authorities involved: from the civil servant negotiating the agreement to the facility operator who has to make his inventory accessible to IAEA inspectors. This cooperation will continue to be needed wherever and as long as safeguards will be applied. The Agency has to earn it constantly, by employing a professionally competent approach, tact, discretion and—perhaps most importantly—by never asking for more information than it demonstrably needs. *Safeguards cannot be imposed.* They can only be made possible by continuing mutual agreement at every level.

With regard to future prospects, the viability of the Non-Proliferation Treaty will largely depend on considerations other than safeguards. International safeguards will survive. They will be called for to an ever greater degreee, as a condition of international nuclear trade. The Agency's safeguards system works, although there is room for improvement. The basic documents are working propositions. The document more recently developed in the special context of the NPT, being the more specific of the two, affords better protection of states' interests. In covering all peaceful nuclear activities of the state, it is also much more relevant to the concept of non-proliferation which is basic to all safeguards arrangements. INFCIR/153 has already been used once outside the framework of the NPT, for a state requesting Agency safeguards as a party to the Tlatelolco Treaty. It may well be worth considering whether—in the extreme case that there is no further significant adherence to the NPT—and updated version of INFCIRC/66/Rev.2, revised in the light of INFCIRC/153, could not be used as the basis for future safeguards agreements.

References

1. See, for example, press briefing by US Department of State officers on 14 June 1974. However, see also pp. 19–20.
2. Imai, Ryukichi, *Nuclear Safeguards*, Adelphi Paper Paper No. 86 (London, The International Institute of Strategic Studies, March 1972), p. 10 *et. seq.*
3. INFCIRC/66/Rev.2, paragraph 8.

Appendix 1

I. *Annex 1. Extracts from IAEA document INFCIRC/209, 3 September 1974 and INFCIRC/209/Add. 2, 24 October 1974*

The export of nuclear material and of certain categories of equipment and other material

Communications dated 22 August 1974

1. On 22 August 1974 the Director General received letters, all dated that day, from the Resident Representatives to the Agency of Australia, Denmark Canada, Finland, Norway, the Union of Soviet Socialist Republics, the United Kingdom of Great Britain and Northern Ireland and the United States of America, relating to the commitments of these eight Members under Article III, paragraph 2 of the Treaty on the Non-Proliferation of Nuclear Weapons. In the light of the wish expressed at the end of each of those letters, their text is reproduced below as Letter I. Similar communications have since been made by the Representatives of the German Democratic Republic, Hungary and Poland.

2. On the same day, the Resident Representatives of Denmark and of the United Kingdom also addressed complementary letters to the Director General, the text of which is reproduced below as Letter II. On that day also the Resident Representative of the United States sent a complementary letter, the text of which is reproduced as Letter III.

3. Also on 22 August, the Resident Representatives of the Federal Republic of Germany and of the Netherlands each addressed to the Director General a letter analogous to the above-mentioned Letters I and II, the text of which is reproduced below as Letter IV.

4. The attachments to the Letters I and IV, which consist in both cases of the same memoranda, are reproduced in the Appendix. [See below.]

Letter I

I have the honour to inform you that the Government of . . . has had under consideration procedures in relation to exports of (a) source or special fissionable material, and (b) equipment and material especially designed or prepared for the processing, use or production of special fissionable material, in the light of its commitment under Article III paragraph 2 of the Treaty on the Non-Proliferation of Nuclear Weapons not to provide such items to any non-nuclear-weapon State for peaceful purposes, unless the source or special fissionable material is subject to safeguards under an agreement with the International Atomic Energy Agency.

The Government of . . . has decided to act in this context in accordance with the attached memoranda.

I shall be grateful if you will bring this information to the attention of all Members of the Agency.

Letter II

I have the honour to refer to my letter of today's date, and to inform you that, so far as trade within the European Community is concerned, the Government of . . . will, where necessary, implement paragraphs 5 of the memoranda enclosed with that letter in the light of its commitments under the Treaties of Rome.

Letter III

With reference to my letter of this date, concerning procedures of the Government of the United States of America in relation to exports of source and special fissionable material and of equipment and material especially designed or prepared for the processing, use or production of special fissionable material, I shall provide you shortly with additional information concerning the implementation by my Government of such procedures.

I would like to call attention to paragraph 6 of Memorandum B, enclosed with my letter, and to note that, in accordance with existing procedures of my Government, safeguards are required in relation to items of equipment and material exported from the United States of America, in addition to those specified in paragraph 2 of that Memorandum.

I shall be grateful if you will bring this information to the attention of all Members of the Agency.

Letter IV

I have the honour to inform you that the Government of . . . has had under consideration procedures in relation to exports to any non-nuclear-weapon State for peaceful purposes of (a) source or special fissionable material, and (b) certain categories of equipment and material especially designed or prepared for the processing, use or production of special fissionable material.

The Government of . . . has decided to act in this context in accordance with the attached memoranda. So far as trade within the European Community is concerned, the Government of . . . will, where necessary, implement paragraphs 5 of the memoranda in the light of its commitments under the Treaties of Rome.

I shall be grateful if you will bring this information to the attention of all Members of the Agency.

Memorandum A

INTRODUCTION

1. The Government has had under consideration procedures in relation to exports of nuclear materials in the light of its commitment not to provide source or special fissionable material to any non-nuclear-weapon State for peaceful purposes unless the source or special fissionable material is subject to safeguards under an agreement with the International Atomic Energy Agency.

DEFINITION OF SOURCE AND SPECIAL FISSIONABLE MATERIAL

2. The definition of source and special fissionable material adopted by the Government shall be that contained in Article XX of the Agency's Statute.

THE APPLICATION OF SAFEGUARDS

3. The Government is solely concerned with ensuring, where relevant, the

application of safeguards in non-nuclear-weapon States not party to the Treaty on the Non-Proliferation of Nuclear Weapons (NPT) with a view to preventing diversion of the safeguarded nuclear material from peaceful purposes to nuclear weapons or other nuclear explosive devices. If the Government wishes to supply source or special fissionable material for peaceful purposes to such a State, it will:

(a) Specify to the recipient State, as a condition of supply, that the source or special fissionable material, or special fissionable material produced in or by the use thereof, shall not be diverted to nuclear weapons or other nuclear explosive devices; and

(b) Satisfy itself that safeguards to that end, under an agreement with the Agency and in accordance with its safeguards system, will be applied to the source or special fissionable material in question.

DIRECT EXPORTS

4. In the case of direct exports of source or special fissionable material to non-nuclear-weapon States not party to NPT, the Government will satisfy itself, before authorizing the export of the material in question, that such material will be subject to a safeguards agreement with the Agency, as soon as the recipient State takes over responsibility for the material, but no later than the time the material reaches its destination.

RETRANSFERS

5. The Government, when exporting source or special fissionable material to a nuclear-weapon State not party to NPT, will require satisfactory assurances that the material will not be re-exported to a non-nuclear-weapon State not party to NPT unless arrangements corresponding to those referred to above are made for the acceptance of safeguards by the State receiving such re-export.

MISCELLANEOUS

6. Exports of the items specified in sub-paragraph (a) below, and exports of source or special fissionable material to a given recipient country, within a period of 12 months, below the limits specified in sub-paragraph (b) below, shall be disregarded for the purpose of the procedures described above:

(a) Plutonium with an isotopic concentration of plutonium-238 exceeding 80 %; Special fissionable material when used in gram quantities or less as a sensing component in instruments; and
Source material which the Government is satisfied is to be used only in non-nuclear activities, such as the production of alloys or ceramics;

(b) Special fissionable material   50 effective grams;
Natural uranium   500 kilograms;
Depleted uranium   1 000 kilograms; and
Thorium   1 000 kilograms.

Memorandum B

INTRODUCTION

1. The Government has had under consideration procedures in relation to exports of certain categories of equipment and material, in the light of its commitment not to provide equipment or material especially designed or prepared for the processing,

use or production of special fissionable material to any non-nuclear-weapon State for peaceful purposes, unless the source or special fissionable material produced, processed or used in the equipment or material in question is subject to safeguards under an agreement with the International Atomic Energy Agency.

THE DESIGNATION OF EQUIPMENT OR MATERIAL ESPECIALLY DESIGNED OR PREPARED FOR THE PROCESSING, USE OR PRODUCTION OF SPECIAL FISSIONABLE MATERIAL

2. The designation of items of equipment or material especially designed or prepared for the processing, use or production of special fissionable material (hereinafter referred to as the "Trigger List") adopted by the Government is as follows (quantities below the indicated levels being regarded as insignificant for practical purposes):

2.1 *Reactors and equipment therefor:*

2.1.1. Nuclear reactors capable of operation so as to maintain a controlled self-sustaining fission chain reaction, excluding zero energy reactors, the latter being defined as reactors with a designed maximum rate of production of plutonium not exceeding 100 grams per year.

2.1.2. Reactor pressure vessels:

Metal vessels, as complete units or as major shop-fabricated parts therefor, which are especially designed or prepared to contain the core of a nuclear reactor as defined in paragraph 2.1.1 above and are capable of withstanding the operating pressure of the primary coolant.

2.1.3. Reactor fuel charging and discharging machines:

Manipulative equipment especially designed or prepared for inserting or removing fuel in a nuclear reactor as defined in paragraph 2.1.1 above capable of on-load operation or employing technically sophisticated positioning or alignment features to allow complex off-load fuelling operations such as those in which direct viewing of or access to the fuel is not normally available.

2.1.4. Reactor control rods:

Rods especially designed or prepared for the control of the reaction rate in a nuclear reactor as defined in paragraph 2.1.1 above.

2.1.5. Reactor pressure tubes:

Tubes which are especially designed or prepared to contain fuel elements and the primary coolant in a reactor as defined in paragraph 2.1.1 above at an operating pressure in excess of 50 atmospheres.

2.1.6. Zirconium tubes:

Zirconium metal and alloys in the form of tubes or assemblies of tubes, and in quantities exceeding 500 kg, especially designed or prepared for use in a reactor as defined in paragraph 2.1.1. above, and in which the relationship of hafnium to zirconium is less than 1:500 parts by weight.

2.1.7. Primary coolant pumps:

Pumps especially designed or prepared for circulating liquid metal as primary coolant for nuclear reactors as defined in paragraph 2.1.1 above.

2.2. *Non-nuclear materials for reactors:*

    2.2.1. Deuterium and heavy water:

        Deuterium and any deuterium compound in which the ratio of deuterium to hydrogen exceeds 1:5000 for use in a nuclear reactor as defined in paragraph 2.1.1 above in quantities exceeding 200 kg of deuterium atoms for any one recipient country in any period of 12 months.

    2.2.2. Nuclear grade graphite:

        Graphite having a purity level better than 5 parts per million boron equivalent and with a density greater than 1.50 grams per cubic centimetre in quantities exceeding 30 metric tons for any one recipient country in any period of 12 months.

    2.3.1. Plants for the reprocessing of irradiated fuel elements, and equipment especially designed or prepared therefor.

    2.4.1. Plants for the fabrication of fuel elements.

    2.5.1. Equipment, other than analytical instruments, especially designed or prepared for the separation of isotopes of uranium.

Clarifications of certain of the items on the above list are annexed.

THE APPLICATION OF SAFEGUARDS

3. The Government is solely concerned with ensuring, where relevant, the application of safeguards in non-nuclear-weapon States not party to the Treaty on the Non-Proliferation of Nuclear Weapons (NPT) with a view to preventing diversion of the safeguarded nuclear material from peaceful purposes to nuclear weapons or other nuclear explosive devices. If the Government wishes to supply Trigger List items for peaceful purposes to such a State, it will:

(*a*) Specify to the recipient State, as a condition of supply, that the source or special fissionable material produced, processed or used in the facility for which the item is supplied shall not be diverted to nuclear weapons or other nuclear explosive devices; and

(*b*) Satisfy itself that safeguards to that end, under an agreement with the Agency and in accordance with its safeguards system, will be applied to the source or special fissionable material in question.

DIRECT EXPORTS

4. In the case of direct exports to non-nuclear-weapon States not party to NPT, the Government will satisfy itself, before authorizing the export of the equipment or material in question, that such equipment or material will fall under a safeguards agreement with the Agency.

RETRANSFERS

5. The Government, when exporting Trigger List items, will require satisfactory assurances that the items will not be re-exported to a non-nuclear-weapon State not party to NPT unless arrangements corresponding to those referred to above are made for the acceptance of safeguards by the State receiving such re-export.

MISCELLANEOUS

6. The Government reserves to itself discretion as to interpretation and implementation of its commitment referred to in paragraph 1 above and the right to require,

if it wishes, safeguards as above in relation to items it exports in addition to those items specified in paragraph 2 above.

Clarifications of items on the Trigger List

A. *Complete nuclear reactors*
(Item 2.1.1 of the Trigger List)

1. A "nuclear reactor" basically includes the items within or attached directly to the reactor vessel, the equipment which controls the level of power in the core, and the components which normally contain or come in direct contact with or control the primary coolant of the reactor core.

2. The export of the whole set of major items within this boundary will take place only in accordance with the procedures of the memorandum. Those individual items within this functionally defined boundary which will be exported only in accordance with the procedures of the memorandum are listed in paragraphs 2.1.1 to 2.1.5. Pursuant to paragraph 6 of the memorandum, the Government reserves to itself the right to apply the procedures of the memorandum to other items within the functionally defined boundary.

3. It is not intendend to exclude reactors which could reasonably be capable of modification to produce significantly more than 100 grams of plutonium per year. Reactors designed for sustained operation at significant power levels, regardless of their capacity for plutonium production, are not considered as "zero energy reactors".

B. *Pressure vessels*
(Item 2.1.2 of the Trigger List)

4. A top plate for a reactor pressure vessel is covered by item 2.1.2 as a major shop-fabricated part of a pressure vessel.

5. Reactor internals (e. g. support columns and plates for the core and other vessel internals, control rod guide tubes, thermal shields, baffles, core grid plates, diffuser plates, etc.) are normally supplied by the reactor supplier. In some cases, certain internal support components are included in the fabrication of the pressure vessel. These items are sufficiently critical to the safety and reliability of the operation of the reactor (and, therefore, to the guarantees and liability of the reactor supplier), so that their supply, outside the basic supply arrangement for the reactor itself, would not be common practice. Therefore, although the separate supply of these unique, especially designed and prepared, critical, large and expensive items would not necessarily be considered as falling outside the area of concern, such a mode of supply is considered unlikely.

C. *Reactor control rods*
(Item 2.1.4 of the Trigger List)

6. This item includes, in addition to the neutron absorbing part, the support or suspension structures therefor if supplied separately.

D. *Fuel reprocessing plants*
(Item 2.3.1 of the Trigger List)

7. A "plant for the reprocessing of irradiated fuel elements" includes the equipment and components which normally come in direct contact with and directly control the irradiated fuel and the major nuclear material and fission product processing streams. The export of the whole set of major items within this

boundary will take place only in accordance with the procedures of the memorandum. In the present state of technology only two items of equipment are considered to fall within the meaning of the phrase "and equipment especially designed or prepared therefor". These items are:

(*a*) Irradiated fuel element chopping machines: remotely operated equipment especially designed or prepared for use in a reprocessing plant as identified above and intended to cut, chop or shear irradiated nuclear fuel assemblies, bundles or rods; and

(*b*) Critically safe tanks (e. g. small diameter, annular or slab tanks) especially designed or prepared for use in a reprocessing plant as identified above, intended for dissolution of irradiated nuclear fuel and which are capable of withstanding hot, highly corrosive liquid, and which can be remotely loaded and maintained.

8. Pursuant to paragraph 6 of the memorandum, the Government reserves to itself the right to apply the procedures of the memorandum to other items within the functionally defined boundary.

E. *Fuel fabrication plants*
(Item 2.4.1 of the Trigger List)

9. A "plant for the fabrication of fuel elements" includes the equipment:

(*a*) Which normally comes in direct contact with, or directly processes, or controls, the production flow of nuclear material, or

(*b*) Which seals the nuclear material within the cladding.

10. The export of the whole set of items for the foregoing operations will take place only in accordance with the procedures of the memorandum. The Government will also give consideration to application of the procedures of the memorandum to individual items intended for any of the foregoing operations, as well as for other fuel fabrication operations, such as checking the integrity of the cladding or the seal, and the finish treatment to the solid fuel.

F. *Isotope separation plant equipment*
(Item 2.5.1 of the Trigger List)

11. "Equipment, other than analytical instruments, especially designed or prepared for the separation of isotopes of uranium" includes each of the major items of equipment especially designed or prepared for the separation process.

Further communications dated 3 October 1974

1. On 7 October 1974 the Director General received a letter dated 3 October 1974 from the Resident Representative of the United States of America to the Agency referring to his two letters of 22 August regarding the export of nuclear material and of certain categories of equipment and other material.[1] In the light of the wish expressed at the end of that letter its text is reproduced below as Letter A.

2. On the same day, the Director General also received a letter from the Resident Representative of the Union of Soviet Socialist Republics, dated 3 October 1974, dealing with the same subject. The text of that letter is reproduced below as Letter B.

---

[1] Reproduced in document INFCIRC/209 as Letters I and III.

I have the honour to refer to my letters of 22 August 1974, concerning procedures of my Government in relation to exports of source and special fissionable material and of equipment and material especially designed or prepared for the processing, use or production of special fissionable material.

Deliveries to the European Atomic Energy Community and to its Members of source and special fissionable material and of equipment and material especially designed or prepared for the processing, use or production of special fissionable material, under contracts made pursuant to existing agreements between the United States of America and the European Atomic Energy Community will continue to be made, in the light of our expectation that the agreement between the International Atomic Energy Agency, the European Atomic Energy Community and certain of its Member States, signed on 5 April 1973, will enter into force in the very near future.

With respect to paragraph 3 of each of the memoranda transmitted on 22 August,[2] I wish to note that the representative of the Government of the United States has placed on the record of meetings of the Board of Governors of the Agency held on 1 March 1972 and on 12 June 1974 the understanding inherent in all of the bilateral agreements for co-operation to which the Government of the United States is a party, that the use of any material or equipment supplied by the United States under such agreements for any nuclear explosive device is precluded; and the understanding inherent in the safeguards agreements related to such co-operation agreements, that the Agency would verify, inter alia, that the safeguarded material was not used for any nuclear explosive device. It was further noted by the United States representative that the continued co-operation of the United States with other countries in the nuclear field is dependent on the assurance that these understandings will continue to be respected in the future.

I shall be grateful if you will bring this information to the attention of all Members of the Agency.

Letter B

The Soviet Union is scrupulously fulfilling its obligations under the Treaty on the Non-Proliferation of Nuclear Weapons (NPT), Article I of which, as we know, provides inter alia that nuclear-weapon States party to the Treaty must 'not in any way ... assist, encourage or induce any non-nuclear-weapon State to manufacture or otherwise acquire nuclear weapons or other nuclear explosive devices'. This obligation applies in full to the supply to any non-nuclear-weapon State of the equipment and materials mentioned in Article III.2 of the Treaty, which may not be used in those countries for the manufacture of nuclear weapons or other nuclear explosive devices.

In connection with the entry into force of the safeguards machinery referred to in Article III.2 of NPT, we deem it necessary to emphasize once more the importance of the speediest possible completion of the process of accession to the Treaty by the countries members of the European Atomic Energy Community which have signed it, and of the entry into force of the appropriate Safeguards Agreement with the Agency.

---

[2] Reproduced in document INFCIRC/209, Appendix, as Memoranda A and B.

II. *Annex 2. Arrangements for the financing of safeguards*

1. The Director General shall make an initial determination of the base rate of assessment for each Member State. This shall be based on the scale adopted by the United Nations in assessing contributions of Member States to the Regular Budget of the United Nations, adjusted for differences in membership between the United Nations and the Agency.

2. The administrative expenses of the Agency shall be divided into:

(*a*) Non-safeguards expenses, which shall include all expenses required to be apportioned among Members in accordance with Article XIV.D of the Statute, except costs relating to the safeguards activities of the Agency; and

(*b*) Safeguards expenses, which shall include all costs relating to the safeguards activities of the Agency.

3. The General Conference shall apply the following provisions in fixing the scale of assessments under Article XIV.D of the Statute:

(*a*) Non-safeguards expenses shall be borne by Members in proportion to their base rates of assessment;

(*b*) Safeguards expenses, after deduction of such amounts as are recoverable under agreements with the Agency relating to safeguards in respect of parties thereto which are not Members of the Agency, shall be borne by Members as follows:

   (i) No Member shall pay less than an amount determined by applying its base rate of assessment for 1971[1] to the safeguards section of the Regular Budget for 1971.[2]

   (ii) Subject to sub-paragraph (i) above, each Member on the list[3] to be drawn up by the Director General shall either bear a share corresponding to one half of its base rate of assessment or pay 16.9 % of the amount it bears under sub-paragraph (*a*) above, whichever is the less; and

   (iii) All other Members shall contribute on a scale to be determined by applying a proportionate increase to their base rates of assessment sufficient to make up the balance of the safeguards expenses.

4. Agency safeguards agreements relating to parties thereto which are not Members of the Agency shall provide for full reimbursement to the Agency of the safeguards expenses it incurs thereunder.

5. The Board shall review the arrangements set out in sub-paragraph 3 (*b*) above at an appropriate time after 1975.

---

[1] See General Conference Resolution GC(XIV)/RES/267, paragraph 1.

[2] Resolution GC(XIV)/RES/264, paragraph 1.

[3] The method by which the list is to be drawn up is specified in Paragraph C(ii) of resolution GC(XV)/RES/283; it has to comprise Members, except those that have notified the Director General that they do not wish to be included, having *per capita* net national products of less than one third of the average *per capita* national products of the ten Members having the highest *per capita* net national products, the *per capita* net national products being identified by examination of the documents used by the Committee on Contributions of the General Assembly of the United Nations.

Appendix 2

The members of the International Atomic Energy Agency

On 1 November 1974 the Members of the Agency were the 105 States listed below:

Afghanistan
Albania
Algeria
Argentina
Australia
Austria
Bangladesh
Belgium
Bolivia
Brazil
Bulgaria
Burma
Byelorussian Soviet
  Socialist Republic
Cameroon
Canada
Chile
Colombia
Costa Rica
Cuba
Cyprus
Czechoslovak Socialist
  Republic
Democratic People's
  Republic of Korea
Denmark
Dominican Republic
Ecuador
Egypt, Arab Republic of
El Salvador
Ethiopia
Finland
France
Gabon
German Democratic
  Republic
Germany, Federal
  Republic of

Ghana
Greece
Guatemala
Haiti
Holy See
Hungary
Iceland
India
Indonesia
Iran
Iraq
Ireland
Israel
Italy
Ivory Coast
Jamaica
Japan
Jordan
Kenya
Khmer Republic
Korea, Republic of
Kuwait
Lebanon
Liberia
Libyan Arab Republic
Liechtenstein
Luxembourg
Madagascar
Malaysia
Mali
Mexico
Monaco
Mongolia
Morocco
Netherlands
New Zealand
Niger
Nigeria

Norway
Pakistan
Panama
Paraguay
Peru
Philippines
Poland
Portugal
Romania
Saudi Arabia
Senegal
Sierra Leone
Singapore
South Africa
Spain
Sri Lanka
Sudan
Sweden
Switzerland
Syrian Arab Republic
Thailand
Tunisia
Turkey
Uganda
Ukrainian Soviet Socialist
  Republic
Union of Soviet Socialist
  Republics
United Kingdom of Great
  Britain and Northern Ireland
United States of America
Uruguay
Venezuela
Viet-Nam
Yugoslavia
Zaire, Republic of
Zambia

Appendix 2 A

Situation on 31 December 1974 with respect to the signature of, ratification of, or accession to the NPT by non-nuclear-weapon States, and the conclusion of safeguards agreements between the Agency and these States in connection with the NPT*

Non-nuclear-weapon States which have signed, ratified or acceded to NPT	Date of ratification or accession	Safeguards agreement with the Agency
Afghanistan	4 February 1970	Under negotiation
Australia	23 January 1973	In force: 10 July 1974
Austria	28 June 1969	In force: 23 July 1972
Barbados		Under negotiation
Belgium		Signed: 5 April 1973
Bolivia	26 May 1970	Signed: 23 August 1974
Botswana	28 April 1969	Under negotiation
Bulgaria	5 September 1969	In force: 29 February 1972
Burundi	19 March 1971	
Cameroon	8 January 1969	
Canada	8 January 1969	In force: 21 February 1972
Central African Republic	25 October 1970	
Chad	10 March 1971	
China, Republic of	27 January 1970	Negotiation discontinued
Colombia		
Costa Rica	3 March 1970	Signed: 12 July 1973
Cyprus	16 February 1970	In force: 26 January 1973
Czechoslovak Socialist Republic	22 July 1969	In force: 3 March 1972
Dahomey	31 October 1972	
Denmark	3 January 1969	In force: 1 March 1972
Dominican Republic	24 July 1971	In force: 11 October 1973
Ecuador	7 March 1969	Signed: 2 October 1974
Egypt, Arab Republic of		
El Salvador	11 July 1972	Approved by the Board
Ethiopia	5 February 1970	Under negotiation
Fiji	14 July 1972	In force: 22 March 1973
Finland	5 February 1969	In force: 9 February 1972
Gabon	19 February 1974	Under negotiation
Gambia		
German Democratic Republic	31 October 1969	In force: 7 March 1972
Germany, Federal Republic of		Signed: 5 April 1973
Ghana	5 May 1970	Signed: 23 August 1973
Greece	11 March 1970	Provisionally in force: 1 March 1972
Guatamala	22 September 1970	Under negotiation
Haiti	2 June 1970	Approved by the Board
Holy See	25 February 1971	In force: 1 August 1972
Honduras	16 May 1973	Approved by the Board
Hungary	27 May 1969	In force: 20 March 1972

* An entry in the first column of this list does not imply the expression of any opinion concerning the legal status of any country or territory or of its authorities, or concerning the delimitation of its frontiers.

Non-nuclear-weapon States which have signed, ratified or acceded to NPT	Date of ratification or accession	Safeguards agreement with the Agency
Iceland	18 July 1969	In force: 16 October 1974
Indonesia		
Iran	2 February 1970	In force: 15 May 1974
Iraq	29 October 1969	In force: 29 February 1972
Ireland	1 July 1968	In force: 29 February 1972
Italy		Signed: 5 April 1973
Ivory Coast	6 March 1973	
Jamaica	5 March 1970	Under negotiation
Japan		
Jordan	11 February 1970	Approved by the Board
Kenya	11 July 1970	Under negotiation
Khmer Republic	2 June 1972	
Korea, Republic of		
Kuwait		
Laos	20 February 1970	Under negotiation
Lebanon	15 July 1970	In force: 5 March 1973
Lesotho	20 May 1970	In force: 12 June 1973
Liberia	5 March 1970	
Libyan Arab Republic		
Luxembourg		Signed: 5 April 1973
Madagascar	8 October 1970	In force: 14 June 1973
Malaysia	5 March 1970	In force: 29 February 1972
Maldives	7 April 1970	Under negotiation
Mali	5 March 1970	Under negotiation
Malta	6 February 1970	Under negotiation
Mauritius	28 April 1969	In force: 31 January 1973
Mexico	21 January 1969	In force: 14 September 1973
Mongolia	14 May 1969	In force: 5 September 1972
Morocco	30 November 1970	Signed: 30 January 1973
Nepal	5 January 1970	In force: 22 June 1972
Netherlands[b]		Signed: 5 April 1973
New Zealand	10 September 1969	In force: 29 February 1972
Nicaragua	6 March 1973	Approved by the Board
Nigeria	27 September 1968	Under negotiation
Norway	5 February 1969	In force: 1 March 1972
Panama		
Paraguay	4 February 1970	
Peru	3 March 1970	Under negotiation
Philippines	5 October 1972	In force: 16 October 1974
Poland	12 June 1969	In force: 11 October 1972
Romania	4 February 1970	In force: 27 October 1972
San Marino	10 August 1970	Under negotiation
Senegal	17 December 1970	Under negotiation
Sierra Leone[a]		Under negotiation
Singapore		
Somalia	5 March 1970	Under negotiation
Southern Yemen		
Sudan	31 October 1973	
Sri Lanka		
Swaziland	11 December 1969	Approved by the Board
Sweden	9 January 1970	Under negotiation
Switzerland		Under negotiation
Syrian Arab Republic	24 September 1969	
Thailand	7 December 1972	In force: 16 May 1974
Togo	26 February 1970	
Tonga	7 July 1971	Under negotiation

Non-nuclear-weapon States which have signed, ratified or acceded to NPT	Date of ratification or accession	Safeguards agreement with the Agency
Trinidad and Tobago		
Tunisia	26 February 1970	Under negotiation
Turkey		
Upper Volta	3 March 1970	
Uruguay	31 August 1970	Signed: 24 September 1971
Venezuela		
Viet-Nam	10 September 1971	In force: 9 January 1974
Yemen, Arab Republic of		
Yugoslavia	3 March 1970	In force: 28 December 1973
Zaire, Republic of	4 August 1970	In force: 9 November 1972

[a] Has not acceded to NPT.

[b] The Netherlands have also signed, on 5 April 1973, agreements in respect of the Netherlands Antilles and Surinam, under the NPT and the Treaty for the Prohibition of Nuclear Weapons in Latin America.

Appendix 2 B

Agreements providing for safeguards other than those in connection with the NPT, approved by the Board as of 31 December 1974

Party(ies)	Subject	Entry into force	IAEA Ref. Doc. (INFCIRC)
Project agreements			
Argentina	Siemens SUR-100	13 Mar 1970	143
	RAEP Reactor	2 Dec 1964	62
Chile	Herald Reactor	19 Dec 1969	137
Finland[a]	FIR-1 Reactor	30 Dec 1960	24
	FINN sub-critical assembly	30 Jul 1963	53
Greece[a]	GRR-1 Reactor	1 Mar 1972	163
Indonesia	Additional core-load for Triga Reactor	19 Dec 1969	136
Iran[a]	UTRR Reactor	10 May 1967	97
Japan	JRR-3	24 Mar 1959	3
Mexico[a]	TRIGA-III Reactor	18 Dec 1963	52
	Siemens SUR-100	21 Dec 1971	162
	Laguna Verde Nucelar Power Plant	12 Feb 1974	203
Pakistan	PRR Reactor	5 Mar 1962	34
	Booster rods for KANUPP	17 Jun 1968	116
Philippines[a]	PRR-1 Reactor	28 Sep 1966	88
Romania[a]	TRIGA Reactor	30 Mar 1973	206
Spain	Coral 1 Reactor	23 Jun 1967	99
Turkey	Sub-critical assembly	17 May 1974	
Uruguay	URR Reactor	24 Sep 1965	67
Viet-Nam[a]	VNR-1 Reactor	16 Oct 1967	106
Yugoslavia[a]	TRIGA-II Reactor	4 Oct 1961	32
	KRSKO Nuclear Power Plant	14 Jun 1974	213
Zaire, Republic of[a]	TRICO Reactor	27 Jun 1962	37

Transfer agreements

(Agreements for transfer of safeguards under bilateral cooperation agreements between the indicated parties)

Argentina/USA		25 Jul 1969	130
Australia[a]/USA		26 Sep 1966	91
Australia[a]/Japan		28 Jul 1972	170/Corr. 1
Austria[a]/USA		24 Jan 1970	152
Brazil/USA		20 Sep 1972	110/Mod. 1
Canada/Japan		12 Nov 1969	85/Mod. 1
Canada/India		30 Sep 1971	211
China, Republic of/USA		6 Dec 1971	158
Colombia/USA		9 Dec 1970	144
Denmark[a]/UK		23 Jun 1965	63
Denmark[a]/USA		29 Feb 1968	112
France/Japan		22 Sep 1972	171
Greece[a]/USA		13 Jan 1966	78

Transfer agreements (contd.)

India/USA		27 Jan 1971	154
Indonesia/USA		6 Dec 1967	109
Iran[a]/USA		20 Aug 1969	127
Israel/USA		15 Jun 1966	84
Japan/USA		10 Jul 1968	119
Japan/UK		15 Oct 1968	125
Korea/USA		19 Mar 1973	111/Mod. 1
Pakistan/Canada		17 Oct 1969	135
Philippines[a]/USA		19 Jul 1968	120
Portugal/USA		19 Jul 1969	131
South Africa/USA		28 Jun 1974	98
Spain/USA		28 Jun 1974	92
Sweden/USA		1 Mar 1972	165
Switzerland/USA		28 Feb 1972	161
Thailand[a]/USA		10 Sep 1965	68
Turkey/USA		5 Jun 1969	123
Venezuela/USA		27 Mar 1968	122
Viet-Nam[a]/USA		25 Oct 1965	71

Unilateral submissions

Argentina	Atucha Power Reactor Facility	3 Oct 1972	168
	Nuclear Material	23 Oct 1973	202
	Embalse Power Reactor Facility	6 Dec 1974	
Chile	Nuclear Material		
China, Republic of	Taiwan Research Reactor Facility	13 Oct 1969	133
Mexico[a]	All nuclear activities	6 Sep 1968	118
Panama[b]	All nuclear activities		
Spain	Nuclear Material	19 Nov 1974	
United Kingdom	Certain nuclear activities	14 Dec 1972	175

[a] Application of Agency safeguards under this agreement has been suspended as the State has concluded an agreement in connection with NPT.

[b] At present Panama has no significant nuclear activities. The Agreement is concluded under Article 13 of the Treaty for the Prohibition of Nuclear Weapons in Latin America.

Appendix 3

INFCIRC/153, the "Blue Book"

The structure and content of agreements between the Agency and states required in connection with the Treaty on the Non-Proliferation of Nuclear weapons.

Part I

Basic undertaking

1. The Agreement should contain, in accordance with Article III.1 of the Treaty on the Non-Proliferation of Nuclear Weapons, an undertaking by the State to accept safeguards, in accordance with the terms of the Agreement, on all source or special fissionable material in all peaceful nuclear activities within its territory, under its jurisdiction or carried out under its control anywhere, for the exclusive purpose of verifying that such material is not diverted to nuclear weapons or other nuclear explosive devices.

Application of safeguards

2. The Agreement should provide for the Agency's right and obligation to ensure that safeguards will be applied, in accordance with the terms of the Agreement, on all source or special fissionable material in all peaceful nuclear activities within the territory of the State, under its jurisdiction or carried out under its control anywhere, for the exclusive purpose of verifying that such material is not diverted to nuclear weapons or other nuclear explosive devices.

Co-operation between the Agency and the State

3. The Agreement should provide that the Agency and the State shall co-operate to facilitate the implementation of the safeguards provided for therein.

Implementation of safeguards

4. The Agreement should provide that safeguards shall be implemented in a manner designed:

(*a*) To avoid hampering the economic and technological development of the State or international co-operation in the field of peaceful nuclear activities, including international exchange of *nuclear material*[1] ;

(*b*) To avoid undue interference in the State's peaceful nuclear activities, and in particular in the operation of *facilities*, and

(*c*) To be consistent with prudent management practices required for the economic and safe conduct of nuclear activities.

5. The Agreement should provide that the Agency shall take every precaution to protect commercial and industrial secrets and other confidential information coming to its knowledge in the implementation of the Agreement. The Agency shall not publish or communicate to any State, organization or person any information obtained by it in connection with the implementation of the Agreement, except that specific information relating to such implementation in the State may be given to the Board of Governors and to such Agency staff members as require such

---

[1] Terms in italics have specialized meanings, which are defined in paragraphs 98–116 below.

knowledge by reason of their official duties in connection with safeguards, but only to the extent necessary for the Agency to fulfil its responsibilities in implementing the Agreement. Summarized information on *nuclear material* being safeguarded by the Agency under the Agreement may be published upon decision of the Board if the States directly concerned agree.

6. The Agreement should provide that in implementing safeguards pursuant thereto the Agency shall take full account of technological developments in the field of safeguards, and shall make every effort to ensure optimum cost-effectiveness and the application of the principle of safeguarding effectively the flow of *nuclear material* subject to safeguards under the Agreement by use of instruments and other techniques at certain *strategic points* to the extent that present or future technology permits. In order to ensure optimum cost-effectiveness, use should be made, for example, of such means as:

(a) Containment as a means of defining *material balance areas* for accounting purposes;

(b) Statistical techniques and random sampling in evaluating the flow of *nuclear material*; and

(c) Concentration of verification procedures on those stages in the nuclear fuel cycle involving the production, processing, use or storage of *nuclear material* from which nuclear weapons or other nuclear explosive devices could readily be made, and minimization of verification procedures in respect of other *nuclear material*, on condition that this does not hamper the Agency in applying safeguards under the Agreement.

National system of accounting for and control of nuclear material

7. The Agreement should provide that the State shall establish and maintain a system of accounting for and control of all *nuclear material* subject to safeguards under the Agreement, and that such safeguards shall be applied in such a manner as to enable the Agency to verify, in ascertaining that there has been no diversion of *nuclear material* from peaceful uses to nuclear weapons or other nuclear explosive devices, findings of the State's system. The Agency's verification shall include, inter alia, independent measurements and observations conducted by the Agency in accordance with the procedures specified in Part II below. The Agency, in its verification, shall take due account of the technical effectiveness of the State's system.

Provision of information to the Agency

8. The Agreement should provide that to ensure the effective implementation of safeguards thereunder the Agency shall be provided, in accordance with the provisions set out in Part II below, with information concerning *nuclear material* subject to safeguards under the Agreement and the features of *facilities* relevant to safeguarding such material. The Agency shall require only the minimum amount of information and data consistent with carrying out its responsibilities under the Agreement. Information pertaining to *facilities* shall be the minimum necessary for safeguarding *nuclear material* subject to safeguards under the Agreement. In examining design information, the Agency shall, at the request of the State, be prepared to examine on premises of the State design information which the State regards as being of particular sensitivity. Such information would not have to be physically transmitted to the Agency provided that it remained available for ready further examination by the Agency on premises of the State.

Agency inspectors

9. The Agreement should provide that the State shall take necessary steps to

ensure that Agency inspectors can effectively discharge their functions under the Agreement. The Agency shall secure the consent of the State to the designation of Agency inspectors to that State. If the State, either upon proposal of a designation or at any other time after a designation has been made, objects to the designation, the Agency shall propose to the State an alternative designation or designations. The repeated refusal of a State to accept the designation of Agency inspectors which would impede the inspections conducted under the Agreement would be considered by the Board upon referral by the Director General with a view to appropriate action. The visits and activities of Agency inspectors shall be so arranged as to reduce to a minimum the possible inconvenience and disturbance to the State and to the peaceful nuclear activities inspected, as well as to ensure protection of industrial secrets or any other confidential information coming to the inspectors' knowledge.

Privileges and immunities

10. The Agreement should specify the privileges and immunities which shall be granted to the Agency and its staff in respect of their functions under the Agreement. In the case of a State party to the Agreement on the Privileges and Immunities of the Agency, the provisions thereof, as in force for such State, shall apply. In the case of other States, the privileges and immunities granted should be such as to ensure that;

(*a*) The Agency and its staff will be in a position to discharge their functions under the Agreement effectively; and

(*b*) No such State will be placed thereby in a more favourable position than States party to the Agreement on the Privileges and Immunities of the Agency.

Termination of safeguards

Consumption or dilution of nuclear material

11. The Agreement should provide that safeguards shall terminate on *nuclear material* subject to safeguards thereunder upon determination by the Agency that it has been consumed, or has been diluted in such a way that it is no longer usable for any nuclear activity relevant from the point of view of safeguards, or has become practicably irrecoverable.

Transfer of nuclear material out of the State

12. The Agreement should provide, with respect to *nuclear material* subject to safeguards thereunder, for notification of transfers of such material out of the State, in accordance with the provisions set out in paragraphs 92–94 below. The Agency shall terminate safeguards under the Agreement on *nuclear material* when the recipient State has assumed responsibility therefor, as provided for in paragraph 91. The Agency shall maintain records indicating each transfer and, where applicable, the re-application of safeguards to the transferred *nuclear material*.

Provisions relating to nuclear material to be used in non-nuclear activities

13. The Agreement should provide that if the State wishes to use *nuclear material* subject to safeguards thereunder in non-nuclear activites, such as the production of alloys or ceramics, it shall agree with the Agency on the circumstances under which the safeguards on such *nuclear material* may be terminated.

Non-application of safeguards to nuclear material
to be used in non-peaceful activities

14. The Agreement should provide that if the State intends to exercise its discretion to use *nuclear material* which is required to be safeguarded thereunder in

a nuclear activity which. does not require the application of safeguards under the Agreement, the following procedures will apply:

(a) The State shall inform the Agency of the activity, making it clear:

   (i) That the use of the *nuclear material* in a non-proscribed military activity will not be in conflict with an undertaking the State may have given and in respect of which Agency safeguards apply, that the *nuclear material* will be used only in a peaceful nuclear activity; and

   (ii) That during the period of non-applicaton of safeguards the *nuclear material* will not be used for the production of nuclear weapons or other nuclear explosive devices;

(b) The Agency and the State shall make an arrangement so that, only while the *nuclear material* is in such an activity, the safeguards provided for in the Agreement will not be applied. The arrangement shall identify, to the extent possible, the period or circumstances during which safeguards will not be applied. In any event, the safeguards provided for in the Agreement shall again apply as soon as the *nuclear material* is reintroduced into a peaceful nuclear activity. The Agency shall be kept informed of the total quantity and composition of such unsafeguarded *nucelar material* in the State and of any exports of such material; and

(c) Each arrangement shall be made in agreement with the Agency. The Agency's agreement shall be given as promptly as possible; it shall only relate to the temporal and procedural provisions, reporting arrangements, etc., but shall not involve any approval or classified knowledge of the military activity or relate to the use of the *nuclear material* therein.

Finance

15. The Agreement should contain one of the following sets of provisions:

(a) An agreement with a Member of the Agency should provide that each party thereto shall bear the expenses it incurs in implementing its responsibilities thereunder. However, if the State or persons under its jurisdiction incur extraordinary expenses as a result of a specific request by the Agency, the Agency shall reimburse such expenses provided that it has agreed in advance to do so. In any case the Agency shall bear the cost of any additional measuring or sampling which inspectors may request; or

(b) An agreement with a party not a Member of the Agency should in application of the provisions of Article XIV.C of the Statute, provide that the party shall reimburse fully to the Agency the safeguards expenses the Agency incurs thereunder. However, if the party or persons under its jurisdiction incur extraordinary expenses as a result of a specific request by the Agency, the Agency shall reimburse such expenses provided that it has agreed in advance to do so.

Third party liability for nuclear damage

16. The Agreement should provide that the State shall ensure that any protection against third party liability in respect of nuclear damage, including any insurance or other financial security, which may be available under its laws or regulations shall apply to the Agency and its officials for the purpose of the implementation of the Agreement, in the same way as that protection applies to nationals of the State.

International responsibility

17. The Agreement should provide that any claim by one party thereto against the other in respect of any damage, other than damage arising out of a nuclear incident,

resulting from the implementation of safeguards under the Agreement, shall be settled in accordance with international law.

Measures in relation to verification of non-diversion

18. The Agreement should provide that if the Board, upon report of the Director General, decides that an action by the State is essential and urgent in order to ensure verification that *nuclear material* subject to safeguards under the Agreement is not diverted to nuclear weapons or other nuclear explosive devices the Board shall be able to call upon the State to take the required action without delay, irrespective of whether procedures for the settlement of a dispute have been invoked.

19. The Agreement should provide that if the Board upon examination of relevant information reported to it by the Director General finds that the Agency is not able to verify that there has been no diversion of *nuclear material* required to be safeguarded under the Agreement to nuclear weapons or other nuclear explosive devices, it may make the reports provided for in paragraph C of Article XII of the Statute and may also take, where applicable, the other measures provided for in that paragraph. In taking such action the Board shall take account of the degree of assurance provided by the safeguards measures that have been applied and shall afford the State every reasonable opportunity to furnish the Board with any necessary reassurance.

Interpretation and application of the agreement and settlement of disputes

20. The Agreement should provide that the parties thereto shall, at the request of either, consult about any question arising out of the interpretation or application thereof.

21. The Agreement should provide that the State shall have the right to request that any question arising out of the interpretation or application thereof be considered by the Board; and that the State shall be invited by the Board to participate in the discussion of any such question by the Board.

22. The Agreement should provide that any dispute arising out of the interpretation or application thereof except a dispute with regard to a finding by the Board under paragraph 19 above or an action taken by the Board pursuant to such a finding which is not settled by negotiation or another procedure agreed to by the parties should, on the request of either party, be submitted to an arbitral tribunal composed as follows: each party would designate one arbitrator, and the two arbitrators so designated would elect a third, who would be the Chairman. If, within 30 days of the request for arbitration, either party has not designated an arbitrator, either party to the dispute may request the President of the International Court of Justice to appoint an arbitrator. The same procedure would apply if, within 30 days of the designation or appointment of the second arbitrator, the third arbitrator had not been elected. A majority of the members of the arbitral tribunal would constitute a quorum, and all decisions would require the concurrence of two arbitrators. The arbitral procedure would be fixed by the tribunal. The decisions of the tribunal would be binding on both parties.

Final clauses

Amendment of the Agreement

23. The Agreement should provide that the parties thereto shall, at the request of either of them, consult each other on amendment of the Agreement. All amendments shall require the agreement of both parties. It might additionally be provided, if convenient to the State, that the agreement of the parties on

amendments to Part II of the Agreement could be achieved by recourse to a simplified procedure. The Director General shall promptly inform all Member States of any amendment to the Agreement.

Suspension of application of Agency safeguards under other agreements

24. Where applicable and where the State desires such a provision to appear, the Agreement should provide that the application of Agency safeguards in the State under other safeguards agreements with the Agency shall be suspended while the Agreement is in force. If the State has received assistance from the Agency for a project, the State's undertaking in the Project Agreement not to use items subject thereto in such a way as to further any military purpose shall continue to apply.

Entry into force and duration

25. The Agreement should provide that it shall enter into force on the date on which the Agency receives from the State written notification that the statutory and constitutional requirements for entry into force have been met. The Director General shall promptly inform all Member States of the entry into force.

26. The Agreement should provide for it to remain in force as long as the State is party to the Treaty on the Non-Proliferation of Nuclear Weapons.

Part II

Introduction

27. The Agreement should provide that the purpose of Part II thereof is to specify the procedures to be applied for the implementation of the safeguards provisions of Part I.

Objective of safeguards

28. The Agreement should provide that the objective of safeguards is the timely detection of diversion of significant quantities of *nuclear material* from peaceful nuclear activities to the manufacture of nuclear weapons or of other nuclear explosive devices or for purposes unknown, and deterrence of such diversion by the risk of early detection.

29. To this end the Agreement should provide for the use of material accountancy as a safeguards measure of fundamental importance, with containment and surveillance as important complementary measures.

30. The Agreement should provide that the technical conclusion of the Agency's verification activities shall be a statement, in respect of each *material balance area*, of the amount of *material unaccounted for* over a specific period, giving the limits of accuracy of the amounts stated.

National system of accounting for and control of nuclear material

31. The Agreement should provide that pursuant to paragraph 7 above the Agency, in carrying out its verification activities, shall make full use of the State's system of accounting for and control of all *nuclear material* subject to safeguards under the Agreement, and shall avoid unnecessary duplication of the State's accounting and control activities.

32. The Agreement should provide that the State's system of accounting for and control of all *nuclear material* subject to safeguards under the Agreement shall be based on a structure of material balance areas, and shall make provision as appropriate and specified in the Subsidiary Arrangements for the establishment of such measures as:

(*a*) A measurement system for the determination of the quantities of *nuclear material* received, produced, shipped, lost or otherwise removed from inventory, and the quantities on inventory;

(*b*) The evaluation of precision and accuracy of measurements and the estimation of measurement uncertainty;

(*c*) Procedures for identifying, reviewing and evaluating differences in shipper/receiver measurements;

(*d*) Procedures for taking a *physical inventory*;

(*e*) Procedures for the evaluation of accumulations of unmeasured inventory and unmeasured losses;

(*f*) A system of records and reports showing, for each *material balance area*, the inventory of *nuclear material* and the changes in that inventory including receipts into and transfers out of the *material balance area*;

(*g*) Provisions to ensure that the accounting procedures and arrangements are being operated correctly; and

(*h*) Procedures for the provision of reports to the Agency in accordance with paragraphs 59–69 below.

Starting point of safeguards

33. The Agreement should provide that safeguards shall not apply thereunder to material in mining or ore processing activities.

34. The Agreement should provide that:

(*a*) When any material containing uranium or thorium which has not reached the stage of the nuclear fuel cycle described in subparagraph (*c*) below is directly or indirectly exported to a non-nuclear-weapon State, the State shall inform the Agency of its quantity, composition and destination, unless the material is exported for specifically non-nuclear-purposes;

(*b*) When any material containing uranium or thorium which has not reached the stage of the nuclear fuel cycle described in sub-paragraph (*c*) below is imported, the State shall inform the Agency of its quantity and composition, unless the material is imported for specifically non-nuclear-purposes; and

(*c*) When any *nuclear material* of composition and purity suitable for fuel fabrication or for being isotopically enriched leaves the plant or the process stage in which it has been produced, or when such *nuclear material* or any other *nuclear material* produced at a later stage in the nuclear fuel cycle, is imported into the State, the *nuclear material* shall become subject to the safeguards procedures specified in the Agreement.

Termination of safeguards

35. The Agreement should provide that safeguards shall terminate on *nuclear material* subject to safeguards thereunder under the conditions set forth in paragraph 11 above. Where the conditions of that paragraph are not met, but the State considers that the recovery of safeguarded *nuclear material* from residues is not for the time being practicable or desirable, the Agency and the State shall consult on the appropriate safeguards measures to be applied. It should further be

provided that safeguards shall terminate on *nuclear material* subject to safeguards under the Agreement under the conditions set forth in paragraph 13 above, provided that the State and the Agency agree that such *nuclear material* is practicably irrecoverable.

Exemptions from safeguards

36. The Agreement should provide that the Agency shall, at the request of the State, exempt *nuclear material* from safeguards, as follows:

(*a*) Special fissionable material, when it is used in gram quantities or less as a sensing component in instruments;

(*b*) *Nuclear material*, when it is used in non-nuclear activities in accordance with paragraph 13 above, if such *nuclear material* is recoverable; and

(*c*) Plutonium with an isotopic concentration of plutonium-238 exceeding 80%.

37. The Agreement should provide that *nuclear material* that would otherwise be subject to safeguards shall be exempted from safeguards at the request of the State, provided that *nuclear material* so exempted in the State may not at any time exceed:

(*a*) One kilogram in total of special fissionable material, which may consist of one of more of the following:

(i) Plutonium;
(ii) Uranium with an *enrichment* of 0.2 (20 %) and above, taken account of by multiplying its weight by its *enrichment;* and
(iii) Uranium with an *enrichment* below 0.2 (20 %) and above that of natural uranium, taken account of by multiplying its weight by five times the square of its *enrichment;*

(*b*) Ten metric tons in total of natural uranium and depleted uranium with an *enrichment* above 0.005 (0,5 %);

(*c*) Twenty metric tons of depleted uranium with an *enrichment* of 0.005 (0,5 %) or below; and

(*d*) Twenty metric tons of thorium;

or such greater amounts as may be specified by the Board of Governors for uniform application.

38. The Agreement should provide that if exempted *nuclear material* is to be processed or stored together with safeguarded *nuclear material*, provision should be made for the re-application of safeguards thereto.

Subsidiary arrangements

39. The Agreement should provide that the Agency and the State shall make Subsidiary Arrangements which shall specify in detail, to the extent necessary to permit the Agency to fulfil its responsibilities under the Agreement in an effective and efficient manner, how the procedures laid down in the Agreement are to be applied. Provision should be made for the possibility of an extension or change of the Subsidiary Arrangements by agreement between the Agency and the State without amendment of the Agreement.

40. It should be provided that the Subsidiary Arrangements shall enter into force at the same time as, or as soon as possible after, the entry into force of the Agreement. The State and the Agency shall make every effort to achieve their entry into force within 90 days of the entry into force of the Agreement, a later date being acceptable only with the agreement of both parties. The State shall provide the Agency promptly with the information required for completing the Subsidiary

Arrangements. The Agreement should also provide that, upon its entry into force, the Agency shall be entitled to apply the procedures laid down therein in respect of the *nuclear material* listed in the inventory provided for in paragraph 41 below.

Inventory

41. The Agreement should provide that, on the basis of the initial report referred to in paragraph 62 below, the Agency shall establish a unified inventory of all *nuclear material* in the State subject to safeguards under the Agreement, irrespective of its origin, and maintain this inventory on the basis of subsequent reports and of the results of its verification activities. Copies of the inventory shall be made available to the State at agreed intervals.

Design information

General

42. Pursuant to paragraph 8 above, the Agreement should stipulate that design information in respect of existing *facilities* shall be provided to the Agency during the discussion of the Subsidiary Arrangements, and that the time limits for the provision of such information in respect of new *facilities* shall be specified in the Subsidiary Arrangements. It should further be stipulated that such information shall be provided as early as possible before *nuclear material* is introduced into a new *facility*.

43. The Agreement should specify that the design information in respect of each *facility* to be made available to the Agency shall include, when applicable:

(a) The identification of the *facility,* stating its general character, purpose, nominal capacity and geographic location, and the name and address to be used for routine business purposes;

(b) A description of the general arrangement of the *facility* with reference, to the extent feasible, to the form, location and flow of *nuclear material* and to the general layout of important items of equipment which use, produce or process *nuclear material*;

(c) A description of features of the *facility* relating to material accountancy, containment and surveillance; and

(d) A description of the existing and proposed procedures at the *facility* for *nuclear material* accountancy and control, with special reference to *material balance areas* established by the operator, measurements of flow and procedures for *physical inventory* taking.

44. The Agreement should further provide that other information relevant to the application of safeguards shall be made available to the Agency in respect of each *facility*, in particular on organizational responsibility for material accountancy and control. It should also be provided that the State shall make available to the Agency supplementary information on the health and safety procedures which the Agency shall observe and with which the inspectors shall comply at the *facility*.

45. The Agreement should stipulate that design information in respect of a modification relevant for safeguards purposes shall be provided for examination sufficiently in advance for the safeguards procedures to be adjusted when necessary.

Purposes of examination of design information

46. The Agreement should provide that the design information made available to the Agency shall be used for the following purposes:

(a) To identify the features of *facilities* and *nuclear material* relevant to the application of safeguards to *nuclear material* in sufficient detail to facilitate verification;

(*b*) To determine *material balance areas* to be used for Agency accounting purposes and to select those *strategic points* which are *key measurement points* and which will be used to determine the *nuclear material* flows and inventories; in determining such *material balance areas* the Agency shall, inter alia, use the following criteria:

(i) The size of the *material balance area* should be related to the accuracy with which the material balance can be established;

(ii) In determining the *material balance area* advantage should be taken of any opportunity to use containment and surveillance to help ensure the completeness of flow measurements and thereby simplify the application of safeguards and concentrate measurement efforts at *key measurement points;*

(iii) A number of *material balance areas* in use at a *facility* or at distinct sites may be combined in one *material balance area* to be used for Agency accounting purposes when the Agency determines that this is consistent with its verification requirements; and

(iv) If the State so requests, a special *material balance area* around a process step involving commercially sensitive information may be established;

(*c*) To establish the nominal timing and procedures for taking of *physical inventory* for Agency accounting purposes;

(*d*) To establish the records and reports requirements and records evaluation procedures;

(*e*) To establish requirements and procedures for verification of the quantity and location of *nuclear material;* and

(*f*) To select appropriate combinations of containment and surveillance methods and techniques and the *strategic points* at which they are to be applied.

It should further be provided that the results of the examination of the design information shall be included in the Subsidiary Arrangements.

Re-examination of design information

47. The Agreement should provide that design information shall be re-examined in the light of changes in operating conditions, of developments in safeguards technology or of experience in the application of verification procedures, with a view to modifying the action the Agency has taken pursuant to paragraph 46 above.

Verification of design information

48. The Agreement should provide that the Agency, in co-operation with the State, may send inspectors to *facilities* to verify the design information provided to the Agency pursuant to paragraphs 42—45 above for the purposes in paragraph 46.

Information in respect of nuclear material outside facilities

49. The Agreement should provide that the following information concerning *nuclear material* customarily used outside *facilities* shall be provided as applicable to the Agency:

(*a*) A general description of the use of the *nuclear material* its geographic location, and the user's name and address for routine business purposes; and

(*b*) A general description of the existing and proposed procedures for *nuclear material* accountancy and control, including organizational responsibility for material accountancy and control.

The Agreement should further provide that the Agency shall be informed on a timely basis of any change in the information provided to it under this paragraph.

50. The Agreement should provide that the information made available to the Agency in respect of *nuclear material* customarily used outside *facilities* may be used, to the extent relevant, for the purposes set out in sub-paragraph 46(b)–(f) above.

Record system

General

51. The Agreement should provide that the establishing a national system of accounting for and control of *nuclear material* as referred to in paragraph 7 above, the State shall arrange that records are kept in respect of each *material balance area*. Provision should also be made that the Subsidiary Arrangements shall describe the records to be kept in respect of each *material balance area*.

52. The Agreement should provide that the State shall make arrangements to facilitate the examination of records by inspectors, particularly if the records are not kept in English, French, Russian or Spanish.

53. The Agreement should provide that the records shall be retained for at least five years.

54. The Agreement should provide that the records shall consist, as appropriate, of:

(a) Accounting records of all *nuclear material* subject to safeguards under the Agreement; and

(b) Operating records for *facilities* containing such *nuclear material*.

55. The Agreement should provide that the system of measurements on which the records used for the preparation of reports are based shall either conform to the latest international standards or be equivalent in quality to such standards.

Accounting records

56. The Agreement should provide that the accounting records shall set forth the following in respect of each *material balance area*:

(a) All *inventory changes,* so as to permit a determination of the *book inventory* at any time;

(b) All measurement results that are used for determination of the *physical inventory*; and

(c) All *adjustments* and *corrections* that have been made in respect of *inventory changes, book inventories* and *physical inventories.*

57. The Agreement should provide that for all *inventory changes* and *physical inventories* the records shall show, in respect of each *batch* of *nuclear material:* material identification, *batch data* and *source data*. Provision should further be included that records shall account for uranium, thorium and plutonium separately in each *batch* of *nuclear material*. Furthermore, the date of the *inventory change* and, when appropriate, the originating *material balance area* and the receiving *material balance area* or the recipient, shall be indicated for each *inventory change*.

Operating records

58. The Agreement should provide that the operating records shall set forth as appropriate in respect of each *material balance area:*

(*a*) Those operating data which are used to establish changes in the quantities and composition of *nuclear material;*

(*b*) The data obtained from the calibration of tanks and instruments and from sampling and analyses, the procedures to control the quality of measurements and the derived estimates of random and systematic error;

(*c*) A description of the sequence of the actions taken in preparing for, and in taking, a *physical inventory*, in order to ensure that it is correct and complete; and

(*d*) A decription of the actions taken in order to ascertain the cause and magnitude of any accidental or unmeasured loss that might occur.

Reporting system

General

59. The Agreement should specify that the State shall provide the Agency with reports as detailed in paragraphs 60–69 below in respect of *nuclear material* subject to safeguards thereunder.

60. The Agreement should provide that reports shall be made in English, French, Russian or Spanish, except as otherwise specified in the Subsidiary Arrangements.

61. The Agreement should provide that reports shall be based on the records kept in accordance with paragraphs 51–58 above and shall consist, as appropriate, of accounting reports and special reports.

Accounting reports

62. The Agreement should stipulate that the Agency shall be provided with an initial report on all *nuclear material* which is to be subject to safeguards thereunder. It should also be provided that the initial report shall be dispatched by the State to the Agency within 30 days of the last day of the calendar month in which the Agreement enters into force, and shall reflect the situation as of the last day of that month.

63. The Agreement should stipulate that for each *material balance area* the State shall provide the Agency with the following accounting reports:

(*a*) *Inventory change* reports showing changes in the inventory of *nuclear material*. The reports shall be dispatched as soon as possible and in any event within 30 days after the end of the month in which the *inventory changes* occurred or were established; and

(*b*) Material balance report showing the material balance based on a *physical inventory* of *nuclear material* actually present in the *material balance area*. The reports shall be dispatched as soon as possible and in any event within 30 days after the *physical inventory* has been taken.

The reports shall be based on data available as of the date of reporting and may be corrected at a later date as required.

64. The Agreement should provide that *inventory change* reports shall specify identification and *batch data* for each *batch* of *nuclear material*, the date of the *inventory change* and, as appropriate, the originating *material balance area* and the receiving *material balance area* or the recipient. These reports shall be accompanied by concise notes:

(*a*) Explaining the *inventory changes*, on the basis of the operating data contained in the operating records provided for under sub-paragraph 58(*a*) above; and

(*b*) Describing, as specified in the Subsidiary Arrangements, the anticipated operational programme, particularly the taking of a *physical inventory*.

65. The Agreement should provide that the State shall report each *inventory change, adjustment* and *correction* either periodically in a consolidated list or individually. The *inventory changes* shall be reported in terms of *batches;* small amounts, such as analytical samples, as specified in the Subsidiary Arrangements, may be combined and reported as one *inventory change.*

66. The Agreement should stipulate that the Agency shall provide the State with semi-annual statements of *book inventory* of *nuclear material* subject to safeguards, for each *material balance area*, as based on the *inventory change* reports for the period covered by each such statement.

67. The Agreement should specify that the material balance reports shall include the following entries, unless otherwise agreed by the Agency and the State:

(*a*) Beginning *physical inventory;*
(*b*) *Inventory changes* (first increases, then decreases);
(*c*) Ending *book inventory;*
(*d*) *Shipper/receiver differences;*
(*e*) Adjusted ending *book inventory;*
(*f*) Ending *physical inventory;* and
(*g*) *Material unaccounted for.*

A statement of *physical inventory,* listing all *batches* separately and specifying material identification and *batch data* for each *batch,* shall be attached to each material balance report.

Special reports

68. The Agreement should provide that the State shall make special reports without delay:

(*a*) If any unusual incident or circumstances lead the State to believe that there is or may have been loss of *nuclear material* that exceeds the limits to be specified for this purpose in the Subsidiary Arrangements; or
(*b*) If the containment has unexpectedly changed from that specified in the Subsidiary Arrangements to the extent that unauthorized removal of *nuclear material* has become possible.

Amplification and clarification of reports

69. The Agreement should provide that at the Agency's request the State shall supply amplifications or clarifications of any report, in so far as relevant for the purpose of safeguards.

Inspections

General

70. The Agreement should stipulate that the Agency shall have the right to make inspections as provided for in paragraphs 71–82 below.

Purposes of inspections

71. The Agreement should provide that the Agency may make ad hoc inspections in order to:

(*a*) Verify the information contained in the initial report on the *nuclear material* subject to safeguards under the Agreement;
(*b*) Identify and verify changes in the situation which have occurred since the date of the initial report; and
(*c*) Identify, and if possible verify the quantity and composition of, *nuclear*

material in accordance with paragraphs 93 and 96 below, before its transfer out of or upon its transfer into the State.

72. The Agreement should provide that the Agency may make routine inspections in order to:

(*a*) Verify that reports are consistent with records;

(*b*) Verify the location, identity, quantity and composition of all *nuclear material* subject to safeguards under the Agreement; and

(*c*) Verify information on the possible causes of *material unaccounted for, shipper/receiver differences* and uncertainties in the *book inventory*.

73. The Agreement should provide that the Agency may make special inspections subject to the procedures laid down in paragraph 77 below:

(*a*) In order to verify the information contained in special reports; or

(*b*) If the Agency considers that information made available by the State, including explanations from the States and information obtained from routine inspections, is not adequate for the Agency to fulfil its responsibilities under the Agreement.

An inspection shall be deemed to be special when it is either additional to the routine inspection effort provided for in paragraph 78-82 below, or involves access to information or locations in addition to the access specified in paragraph 76 for ad hoc and routine inspections, or both.

Scope of inspections

74. The Agreement should provide that for the purposes stated in paragraphs 71-73 above the Agency may:

(*a*) Examine the records kept pursuant to paragraphs 51-58;

(*b*) Make independent measurements of all *nuclear material* subject to safeguards under the Agreement;

(*c*) Verify the functioning and calibration of instruments and other measuring and control equipment;

(*d*) Apply and make use of surveillance and containment measures; and

(*e*) Use other objective methods which have been demonstrated to be technically feasible.

75. It should further be provided that within the scope of paragraph 74 above the Agency shall be enabled:

(*a*) To observe that samples at *key measurement points* for material balance accounting are taken in accordance with procedures which produce representative samples, to observe the treatment and analysis of the samples and to obtain duplicates of such samples;

(*b*) To observe that the measurements of *nuclear material* at *key measurement points* for material balance accounting are representative, and to observe the calibration of the instruments and equipment involved;

(*c*) To make arrangements with the State that, if necessary:

    (i) Additional measurements are made and additional samples taken for the Agency's use;

    (ii) The Agency's standard analytical samples are analysed;

    (iii) Appropriate absolute standards are used in calibrating instruments and other equipment; and

    (iv) Other calibrations are carried out;

(*d*) To arrange to use its own equipment for independent measurement and surveillance, and if so agreed and specified in the Subsidiary Arrangements to arrange to install such equipment;

(e) To apply its seals and other identifying and tamper-indicating devices to containments, if so agreed and specified in the Subsidiary Arrangements; and

(f) To make arrangements with the State for the shipping of samples taken for the Agency's use.

Access for inspections

76. The Agreement should provide that:

(a) For the purposes specified in sub-paragraphs 71(a) and (b) above and until such time as the *strategic points* have been specified in the Sub-sidiary Arrangements, the Agency's inspectors shall have access to any location where the initial report or any inspections carried out in connection with it indicate that *nuclear material* is present;

(b) For the purposes specified in sub-paragraph 71(c) above the inspectors shall have access to any location of which the Agency has been notified in accordance with sub-paragraphs 92(c) or 95(c) below;

(c) For the purposes specified in paragraph 72 above the Agency's inspectors shall have access only to the *strategic points* specified in the Subsidiary Arrangements and to the records maintained pursuant to paragraphs 51-58; and

(d) In the event of the State concluding that any unusual circumstances require extended limitations on access by the Agency, the State and the Agency shall promptly make arrangements with a view to enabling the Agency to discharge its safeguards responsibilities in the light of these limitations. The Director General shall report each such arrangement to the Board.

77. The Agreement should provide that in circumstances which may lead to special inspections for the purposes specified in paragraph 73 above the State and the Agency shall consult forthwith. As a result of such consultations the Agency may make inspections in addition to the routine inspection effort provided for in paragraphs 78-82 below, and may obtain access in agreement with the State to information or locations in addition to the access specified in paragraph 76 above for ad hoc and routine inspections. Any disagreement concerning the need for additional access shall be resolved in accordance with paragraphs 21 and 22; in case action by the State is essential and urgent, paragraph 18 above shall apply.

Frequency and intensity of routine inspections

78. The Agreement should provide that the number, intensity, duration and timing of routine inspections shall be kept to the minimum consistent with the effective implementation of the safeguards procedures set forth therein, and that the Agency shall make the optimum and most economical use of available inspection resources.

79. The Agreement should provide that in the case of *facilities* and *material balance areas* outside *facilities* with a content or *annual throughput,* whichever is greater, of *nuclear material* not exceeding five *effective kilograms,* routine inspections shall not exceed one per year. For other *facilities* the number, intensity, duration, timing and mode of inspections shall be determined on the basis that in the maximum or limiting case the inspection regime shall be no more intensive than is necessary and sufficient to maintain continuity of knowledge of the flow and inventory of *nuclear material.*

80. The Agreement should provide that the maximum routine inspection effort in respect of *facilities* with a content or *annual throughput* of *nuclear material* exceeding five *effective kilograms* shall be determined as follows:

(a) For reactors and sealed stores, the maximum total of routine inspection per year shall be determined by allowing one sixth of a *man-year of inspections* for each such *facility* in the State;

(b) For other *facilities* involving plutonium or uranium enriched to more than 5%, the maximum total of routine inspection per year shall be determined by allowing for each such *facility* $30x\sqrt{E}$ man-days of inspection per year, where E is the inventory or *annual throughput* of *nuclear material* whichever is greater, expressed in *effective kilograms*. The maximum established for any such *facility* shall not, however, be less than 1.5 *man-years of inspections;* and

(c) For all other *facilities,* the maximum total of routine inspection per year shall be determined by allowing for each such *facility* one third of a *man-year of inspection* plus 0.4 x E man-days of inspection per year, where E is the inventory or *annual throughput* of *nuclear material*, whichever is greater, expressed in *effective kilograms*.

The Agreement should further provide that the Agency and the State may agree to amend the maximum figures specified in this paragraph upon determination by the Board that such amendment is reasonable.

81. Subject to paragraphs 78-80 above the criteria to be used for determining the actual number, intensity, duration, timing and mode of routine inspections of any *facility* shall include:

(a) The form of *nuclear material,* in particular, whether the material is in bulk form or contained in a number of separate items; its chemical composition and, in the case of uranium, whether it is of low or high *enrichment;* and its accessibility;

(b) The effectiveness of the State's accounting and control system, including the extent to which the operators of *facilities* are functionally independent of the State's accounting and control system; the extent to which the measures specified in paragraph 32 above have been implemented by the State; the promptness of reports submitted to the Agency; their consistency with the Agency's independent verification; and the amount and accuracy of the *material unaccounted for,* as verified by the Agency;

(c) Characteristics of the State's nuclear fuel cycle, in particular, the number and types of *facilities* containing *nuclear material* subject to safeguards, the characteristics of such *facilities* relevant to safeguards, notably the degree of containment; the extent to which the design of such *facilities* facilities verification of the flow and inventory of *nuclear material;* and the extent to which information from different *material balance areas* can be correlated;

(d) International interdependence, in particular, the extent to which *nuclear materials* is received from or sent to other States for use or processing; any verification activity by the Agency in connection therewith; and the extent to which the State's nuclear activities are interrelated with those of other States; and

(e) Technical developments in the field of safeguards, including the use of statistical techniques and random sampling in evaluating the flow of *nuclear material.*

82. The Agreement should provide for consultation between the Agency and the State if the latter considers that the inspection effort is being deployed with undue concentration on particular *facilities*.

Notice of inspections

83. The Agreement should provide that the Agency shall give advance notice to the State before arrival of inspectors at *facilities* or *material balance areas* outside

facilities, as follows:

(*a*) For ad hoc inspections pursuant to sub-paragraph 71(*c*) above, at least 24 hours, for those pursuant to sub-paragraph 71(*a*) and (*b*), as well as the activities provided for in paragraph 48; at least one week;

(*b*) For special inspections pursuant to paragraph 73 above, as promptly as possible after the Agency and the State have consulted as provided for in paragraph 77, it being understood that notification of arrival normally will constitute part of the consultations; and

(*c*) For routine inspections pursuant to paragraph 72 above, at least 24 hours in respect of the *facilities* referred to in sub-paragraph 80(*b*) and sealed stores containing plutonium or uranium enriched to more than 5 %, and one week in all other cases.

Such notice of inspections shall include the names of the inspectors and shall indicate the *facilities* and the *material balance areas* outside *facilities* to be visited and the periods during which they will be visited. If the inspectors are to arrive from outside the State the Agency shall also give advance notice of the place and time of their arrival in the State.

84. However, the Agreement should also provide that, as a supplementary measure, the Agency may carry out without advance notification a portion of the routine inspections pursuant to paragraph 80 above in accordance with the principle of random sampling. In performing any unannounced inspections, the Agency shall fully take into account any operational programme provided by the State pursuant to paragraph 64(*b*). Moreover, whenever practicable, and on the basis of the operational programme, it shall advise the State periodically of its general programme of announced and unannounced inspections, specifying the general periods when inspections are foreseen. In carrying out any unannounced inspections, the Agency shall make every effort to minimize any practical difficulties for *facility* operators and the State, bearing in mind the relevant provisions of paragraphs 44 above and 89 below. Similarly the State shall make every effort to facilitate the task of the inspectors.

Designation of inspectors

85. The Agreement should provide that:

(*a*) The Director General shall inform the State in writing of the name, qualifications nationality, grade and such other particulars as may be relevant of each Agency official he proposes for designation as an inspector for the State;

(*b*) The State shall inform the Director General within 30 days of the receipt of such a proposal whether it accepts the proposal;

(*c*) The Director General may designate each official who has been accepted by the State as one of the inspectors for the State, and shall inform the State of such designations; and

(*d*) The Director General, acting in response to a request by the State or on his own initiative, shall immediately inform the State of the withdrawal of the designation of any official as an inspector for the State.

The Agreement should also provide, however, that in respect of inspectors needed for the purposes stated in paragraph 48 above and to carry out ad hoc inspections pursuant to sub-paragraphs 71(*a*) and (*b*) the designation procedures shall be completed if possible within 30 days after the entry into force of the Agreement. If such designation appears impossible within this time limit, inspectors for such purposes shall be designated on a temporary basis.

86. The Agreement should provide that the State shall grant or renew as quickly

as possible appropriate visas, where required, for each inspector designated for the State.

Conduct and visits of inspectors

87. The Agreement should provide that inspectors, in exercising their functions under paragraphs 48 and 71-75 above, shall carry out their activities in a manner designed to avoid hampering or delaying the construction, commissioning or operation of *facilities*, or affecting their safety. In particular inspectors shall not operate any *facility* themselves or direct the staff of a *facility* to carry out any operation. If inspectors consider that in pursuance of paragraphs 74 and 75, particular operations in a *facility* should be carried out by the operator, they shall make a request therefor.

88. When inspectors require services available in the State, including the use of equipment, in connection with the performance of inspections, the State shall facilitate the procurement of such services and the use of such equipment by inspectors.

89. The Agreement should provide that the State shall have the right to have inspectors accompanied during their inspections by representatives of the State, provided that inspectors shall not thereby be delayed or otherwise impeded in the exercise of their functions.

Statements on the Agency's verification activities

90. The Agreement should provide that the Agency shall inform the State of:

(*a*) The results of inspections, at intervals to be specified in the Subsidiary Arrangements; and

(*b*) The conclusions it has drawn from its verification activities in the State, in particular by means of statements in respect of each *material balance areas,* which shall be made as soon as possible after a *physical inventory* has been taken and verified by the Agency and a material balance has been struck.

International transfers

General

91. The Agreement should provide that *nuclear material* subject or required to be subject to safeguards thereunder which is transferred internationally shall, for purposes of the Agreement, be regarded as being the responsibility of the State:

(*a*) In the case of import, from the time that such responsibility ceases to lie with the exporting State, and no later than the time at which the *nuclear material* reaches its destination; and

(*b*) In the case of export, up to the time at which the recipient State assumes such responsibility, and no later than the time at which the *nuclear material* reaches its destination.

The Agreement should provide that the States concerned shall make suitable arrangements to determine the point at which the transfer of responsibility will take place. No State shall be deemed to have such responsibility for *nuclear material* merely by reason of the fact that the *nuclear material* is in transit on or over its territorial waters, or that it is being transported under its flag or in its aircraft.

Transfers out of the State

92. The Agreement should provide that any intended transfer out of the State of

safeguarded *nuclear material* in an amount exceeding one *effective kilogram*, or by successive shipments to the same State within a period of three months each of less than one *effective kilogram* but exceeding in total one *effective kilogram*, shall be notified to the Agency after the conclusion of the contractual arrangements leading to the transfer and normally at least two weeks before the *nuclear material* is to be prepared for shipping. The Agency and the State may agree on different procedures for advance notification. The notification shall specify:

(*a*) The identification and, if possible, the expected quantity and composition of the *nuclear material* to be transferred, and the *material balance area* from which it will come;

(*b*) The State for which the *nuclear material* is destined;

(*c*) The dates on and locations at which the *nuclear material* is to be prepared for shipping;

(*d*) The approximate dates of dispatch and arrival of the *nuclear material*; and

(*e*) At what point of the transfer the recipient State will assume responsibility for the *nuclear material*, and the probable date on which this point will be reached.

93. The Agreement should further provide that the purpose of this notification shall be to enable the Agency if necessary to identify, and if possible verify the quantity and composition of, *nuclear material* subject to safeguards under the Agreement before it is transferred out of the State and, if the Agency so wishes or the State so requests, to affix seals to the *nuclear material* when it has been prepared for shipping. However, the transfer of the *nuclear material* shall not be delayed in any way by any action taken or contemplated by the Agency pursuant to this notification.

94. The Agreement should provide that, if the *nuclear material* will not be subject to Agency safeguards in the recipient State, the exporting State shall make arrangements for the Agency to receive, within three months of the time when the recipient State accepts responsibility for the *nuclear material* from the exporting State, confirmation by the Recipient State of the transfer.

Transfers into the State

95. The Agreement should provide that the expected transfer into the State of *nuclear material* required to be subject to safeguards in an amount greater than one *effective kilogram*, or by successive shipments from the same State within a period of three months each of less than one *effective kilogram* but exceeding in total one *effective kilogram*, shall be notified to the Agency as much in advance as possible of the expected arrival of the *nuclear material*, and in any case not later than the date on which the recipient State assumes responsibility therefor. The Agency and the State may agree on different procedures for advance notification. The notification shall specify:

(*a*) The identification and, if possible, the expected quantity and composition of the *nuclear material*;

(*b*) At what point of the transfer responsibility for the *nuclear material* will be assumed by the State for the purposes of the Agreement, and the probable date on which this point will be reached; and

(*c*) The expected date of arrival, the location to which the *nuclear material* is to be delivered and the date on which it is intended that the *nuclear material* should be unpacked.

96. The Agreement should provide that the purpose of this notification shall be to enable the Agency if necessary to identify, and if possible verify the quantity and composition of, *nuclear material* subject to safeguards which has been

transferred into the State, by means of inspection of the consignment at the time it is unpacked. However, unpacking shall not be delayed by any action taken or contemplated by the Agency pursuant to this notification.

Special reports

97. The Agreement should provide that in the case of international transfers a special report as envisaged in paragraph 68 above shall be made if any unusual incident or circumstances lead the State to believe that there is or may have been loss of *nuclear material*, including the occurence of significant delay during the transfer.

Definitions

98. "Adjustment" means an entry into an accounting record or a report showing a *shipper/receiver difference* or *material unaccounted for*.

99. "Annual throughput" means, for the purposes of paragraphs 79 and 80 above, the amount of *nuclear material* transferred annually out of a *facility* working at nominal capacity.

100. "Batch" means a portion of *nuclear material* handled as a unit for accounting purposes at a *key measurement point* and for which the composition and quantity are defined by a single set of specifications or measurements. The *nuclear material* may be in bulk form or contained in a number of separate items.

101. "Batch data" means the total weight of each element of *nuclear material* and in the case of plutonium and uranium, the isotopic composition when appropriate. The units of account shall be as follows:

(*a*) Grams of contained plutonium;

(*b*) Grams of total uranium and grams of contained uranium-235 plus uranium-233 for uranium-233 for uranium enriched in these isotopes; and

(*c*) Kilograms of contained thorium, natural uranium or depleted uranium.

For reporting purposes the weights of individual items in the *batch* shall be added together before rounding to the nearest unit.

102. "Book inventory" of a *material balance area* means the algebraic sum of the most recent *physical inventory* of that *material balance area* and of all *inventory changes* that have occured since that *physical inventory* was taken.

103. "Correction" means an entry into an accounting record or a report to rectify an identified mistake or to reflect an improved measurement of a quantity previously entered into the record or report. Each correction must identify the entry to which it pertains.

104. "Effective kilogram" means a special unit used in safeguarding *nuclear material*. The quantity in "effective kilograms" is obtained by taking:

(*a*) For plutonium, its weight in kilograms;

(*b*) For uranium with an *enrichment* (of 0.01 (1%) and above, its weight in kilograms multiplied by the square of its *enrichment;*

(*c*) For uranium with an *enrichment* below 0.01 (1%) and above 0.005 (0.5%), its weight in kilograms multiplied by 0.0001; and

(*d*) For depleted uranium with an *enrichment* of 0.005 (0.5%) or below, and for thorium, its weight in kilograms multiplied by 0.00005.

105. "Enrichment" means the ratio of the combined weight of the isotopes uranium-233 and uranium-235 to that of the total uranium in question.

106. "Facility" means:

(*a*) A reactor, a critical facility, a conversion plant, a fabrication plant, a reprocessing plant, an isotope separation plant or a separate storage installation; or

(*b*) Any location where *nuclear material* in amounts greater than one *effective kilogram* is customarily used.

107. "Inventory change" means an increase or decrease, in terms of *batches*, of *nuclear material* in a *material balance area;* such a change shall involve one of this following:

(*a*) Increases:

(i) Import;

(ii) Domestic receipt: receipts from other *material balance areas*, receipts from a non-safeguarded (non-peaceful) activity or receipts at the starting point of safeguards;

(iii) Nuclear production: production of special fissionable material in a reactor; and

(iv) De-exemption: reapplication of safeguards on *nuclear material* previously exempted therefrom on account of its use or quantity.

(*b*) Decreases:

(i) Export;

(ii) Domestic shipment: shipments to other *material balance areas* or shipments for a non-safeguarded (non-peaceful) activity;

(iii) Nuclear loss: loss of *nuclear material* due to its transformation into other element(s) or isotope(s) as a result of nuclear reactions;

(iv) Measured discard: *nuclear material* which has been measured, or estimated on the basis of measurements, and disposed of in such a way that it is not suitable for further nuclear use;

(v) Retained waste: *nuclear material* generated from processing or from an operational accident, which is deemed to be unrecoverable for the time being but which is stored;

(vi) Exemption: exemption of *nuclear material* from safeguards on account of its use or quantity; and

(vii) Other loss: for example, accidental loss (that is, irretrievable and inadvertent loss of *nuclear material* as the result of an operational accident) or theft.

108. "Key measurement point" means a location where *nuclear material* appears in such a form that it may be measured to determine material flow or inventory. "Key measurement points" thus include, but are not limited to, the inputs and outputs (including measured discards) and storages in *material balance areas*.

109. "Man-year of inspection" means, for the purposes of paragraph 80 above, 300 man-days of inspection, a man-day being a day during which a single inspector has access to a *facility* at any time for a total of not more than eight hours.

110. "Material balance area" means an area in or outside of a *facility* such that:

(*a*) The quantity of *nuclear material* in each transfer into or out of each "material balance area" can be determined; and

(*b*) The *physical inventory* of *nuclear material* in each "material balance area" can be determined when necessary, in accordance with specified procedures, in order that the material balance for Agency safeguards purposes can be established.

111. "Material unaccounted for" means the difference between *book inventory* and *physical inventory*.

112. "Nuclear material" means any source or any special fissionable material as defined in Article XX of the Statute. The term source material shall not be

interpreted as applying to ore or ore residue. Any determination by the Board under Article XX of the Statute after the entry into force of this Agreement which adds to the materials considered to be source material or special fissionable material shall have effect under this Agreement only upon acceptance by the State.

113. "Physical inventory" means the sum of all the measured or derived estimates of *batch* quantities of *nuclear material* on hand at a given time within a *material balance area*, obtained in accordance with specified procedures.

114. "Shipper/receiver difference" means the difference between the quantity of *nuclear material* in a *batch* as stated by the shipping *material balance area* and a measured at the receiving *material balance area.*

115. "Source data" means those data, recorded during measurement or calibration or used to derive empirical relationship, which identify *nuclear material* and provide *batch data*. "Source data" may include, for example, weight of compounds, conversion factors to determine weight of element, specific gravity, element concentration, isotopic ratios, relationship between volume and mano-meter readings and relationship between plutonium produced and power generated.

116. "Strategic point" means a location selected during examination of design information where, under normal conditions and when combined with the information from all "strategic points" taken together, the information necessary and sufficient for the implementation of safeguards measures is obtained and verified; a "strategic point" may include any location where key measurements related to material balance accountancy are made and where containment and surveillance measures are executed.

Appendix 4

INFCIRC/66/Rev. 2, 16 September 1968

The Agency's safeguards system (1965, as provisionally extended in 1966 and 1968)

I. *General considerations*

A. The purpose of this document

1. Pursuant to Article II of its Statute the Agency has the task of seeking "to accelerate and enlarge the contribution of atomic energy to peace, health and prosperity throughout the world". Inasmuch as the technology of nuclear energy for peaceful purposes is closely coupled with that for the production of materials for nuclear weapons, the same Article of the Statute provides that the Agency "shall ensure, so far as it is able, that assistance provided by it or at its request or under its supervision or control is not used in such a way as to further any military purpose".

2. The principal purpose of the present document is to establish a system of controls to enable the Agency to comply with this statutory obligation with respect to the activities of Member States in the field of the peaceful uses of nuclear energy, as provided in the Statute. The authority to establish such a system is provided by Article III.A.5. of the Statute, which authorizes the Agency to "establish and administer safeguards designed to ensure that special fissionable and other materials, services, equipment, facilities, and information made available by the Agency or at its request or under its supervision or control are not used in such a way as to further any military purpose". This Article further authorizes the Agency to "apply safeguards, at the request of the parties, to any bilateral or multilateral arrangement, or at the request of a State, to any of that State's activities in the field of atomic energy". Article XII.A sets forth the rights and responsibilities that the Agency is to have, to the extent relevant, with respect to any project or arrangement which it is to safeguard.

3. The principles set forth in this document and the procedures for which it provides are established for the information of Member States, to enable them to determine in advance the circumstances and manner in which the Agency would administer safeguards, and for the guidance of the organs of the Agency itself, to enable the Board and the Director General to determine readily what provisions should be included in agreements relating to safeguards and how to interpret such provisions.

4. Provisions of this document that are relevant to a particular project, arrangement or activity in the field of nuclear energy will only become legally binding upon the entry into force of *a safeguards agreement*[1] and to the extent that they are incorporated therein. Such incorporation may be made by reference.

5. Appropriate provisions of this document may also be incorporated in bilateral or multilateral arrangements between Member States, including all those that

---

[1] The use of italics indicates that a term has a specialized meaning in this document and is defined in Part IV.

provide for the transfer to the Agency of responsibility for administering safeguards system will continue to be administered in accordance with such provisions, unless all States parties thereto request the Agency to substitute the provisions of the present document.

6. Agreements incorporating provisions from the earlier version of the Agency's safeguards system[2] will continue to be administered in accordance with such provisions, unless all States parties thereto request the Agency to substitute the provisions of the present document.

7. Provisions relating to types of *principal nuclear facilities* other then *reactors*, which may produce, process or use safeguarded *nuclear material* will be developed as necessary.

8. The principles and procedures set forth in this document shall be subject to periodic review in the light of the further experience gained by the Agency as well as of technological developments.

B. General principles of the Agency's Safeguards

The Agency's obligations

9. Bearing in mind Article II of the Statute, the Agency shall implement safeguards in a manner designed to avoid hampering a State's economic or technological development.

10. The safeguards procedures set forth in this document shall be implemented in a manner designed to be consistent with prudent management practices required for the economic and safe conduct of nuclear activities.

11. In no case shall the Agency request a State to stop the construction or operation of any *principal nuclear facility* to which the Agency's safeguards procedures extend, except by explicit decision of the Board.

12. The State or States concerned and the Director General shall hold consultations regarding the application of the provisions of the present document.

13. In implementing safeguards, the Agency shall take every precaution to protect commercial and industrial secrets. No member of the Agency's staff shall disclose, except to the Director General and to such other members of the staff as the Director General may authorize to have such information by reason of their official duties in connection with safeguards, any commercial or industrial secret or any other confidential information coming to his knowledge by reason of the implementation of safeguards by the Agency.

14. The Agency shall not publish or communicate to any State, organization or person any information obtained by it in connection with the implementation of safeguards, except that:

(a) Specific information relating to such implementation in a State may be given to the Board and to such Agency staff members as require such knowledge by reason of their official duties in connection with safeguards, but only to the extent necessary for the Agency to fulfil its safeguards responsibilities;

(b) Summarized lists of items being safeguarded by the Agency may be published upon decision of the Board; and

(c) Additional information may be published upon decision of the Board and if all States directly concerned agree.

Principles of implementation

15. The Agency shall implement safeguards in a State if:

(a) The Agency has concluded with the State a *project agreement* under which materials, services, equipment, facilities or information are supplied, and such agreement provides for the application of safeguards; or

(b) The State is a party to a bilateral or multilateral arrangement under which materials, services, equipment, facilities or information are supplied or otherwise transferred, and:

  (i) All the parties to the arrangement have requested the Agency to administer safeguards; and

  (ii) The Agency has concluded the necessary *safeguards agreement* with the State; or

(c) The Agency has been requested by the State to safeguard certain nuclear activities under the latter's jurisdiction, and the Agency has concluded the necessary *safeguards agreement* with the State.

16. In the light of Article XII.A.5 of the Statute, it is desirable that *safeguards agreements* should provide for the continuation of safeguards, subject to the provisions of this document, with respect to produced special fissionable material and to any materials substituted therefor.

17. The principal factors to be considered by the Board in determining the relevance of particular provisions of this document to various types of materials and facilities shall be the form, scope and amount of the assistance supplied, the character of each individual project and the degree to which such assistance could further any military purpose. The related *safeguards agreement* shall take account of all pertinent circumstances at the time of its conclusion.

18. In the event of any non-compliance by a State with a *safeguards agreement*, the Agency may take the measures set forth in Articles XII.A.7 and XII.C of the Statute.

II. *Circumstances requiring safeguards*

A. Nuclear materials subject to safeguards

19. Except as provided in paragraphs 21–28, *nuclear material* shall be subject to the Agency's safeguards if it is being or has been:

(a) Supplied under a *project agreement*; or

(b) Submitted to safeguards under a *safeguards agreement* by the parties to a bilateral or multilateral arrangement; or

(c) *Unilaterally submitted* to safeguards under a *safeguards agreement*; or

(d) Produced, processed or used in a *principal nuclear facility* which has been:

  (i) Supplied wholly or substantially under a *project agreement*; or

  (ii) Submitted to safeguards under a *safeguards agreement* by the parties to a bilateral or multilateral arrangement; or

  (iii) *Unilaterally submitted* to safeguards under a *safeguards agreement*; or

(e) Produced in or by the use of safeguarded *nuclear material*; or

(f) Substituted, pursuant to paragraph 26(d), for safeguarded *nuclear material*.

20. A *principal nuclear facility* shall be considered as substantially supplied under a *project agreement* if the Board has so determined.

B. Exemptions from safeguards

General exemptions

21. *Nuclear material* that would otherwise be subject to safeguards shall be

exempted from safeguards at the request of the State concerned, provided that the material so exempted in that State may not at any time exceed:

(a) 1 kilogram in total of special fissionable material, which may consist of one or more of the following:

    (i) Plutonium;

    (ii) Uranium with an *enrichment* of 0.2 (20 %) and above, taken account of by multiplying its weight by its *enrichment*;

    (iii) Uranium with an *enrichment* below 0.2 (20 %) and above that of natural uranium, taken account of by multiplying its weight by five times the square of its *enrichment*;

(b) 10 metric tons in total of natural uranium and depleted uranium with an *enrichment* above 0.005 (0.5 %);

(c) 20 metric tons of depleted uranium with an *enrichment* of 0.005 (0.5 %) or below; and

(d) 20 metric tons of thorium.

Exemptions related to reactors

22. Produced or used *nuclear material* that would otherwise be subject to safeguards pursuant to paragraph 19(d) or (e) shall be exempted from safeguards if:

(a) It is plutonium produced in the fuel of a *reactor* whose rate of production does not exceed 100 grams of plutonium per year; or

(b) It is produced in a *reactor* determined by the Agency to have a maximum calculated power for continuous operation of less than 3 thermal megawatts, or is used in such a *reactor* and would not be subject to safeguards except for such use, provided that the total power of the *reactors* with respect to which these exemptions apply in any State may not exceed 6 thermal megawatts.

23. Produced special fissionable material that would otherwise be subject to safeguards pursuant only to paragraph 19(e) shall in part be exempted from safeguards if it is produced in a *reactor* in which the ratio of fissionable isotopes within safeguarded *nuclear material* to all fissionable isotopes is less than 0.3 (calculated each time any change is made in the loading of the *reactor* and assumed to be maintained until the next such change). Such fraction of the produced material as corresponds to the calculated ratio shall be subject to safeguards.

C. Suspension of safeguards

24. Safeguards with respect to *nuclear material* may be suspended while the material is transferred, under an arrangement or agreement approved by the Agency, for the purpose of processing, reprocessing, testing, research or development, within the State concerned or to any other Member State or to an international organization, provided that the quantities of *nuclear material* with respect to which safeguards are thus suspended in a State may not at any time exceed;

(a) 1 *effective kilogram* of special fissionable material;

(b) 10 metric tons in total of natural uranium and depleted uranium with an *enrichment* above 0.005 (0.5 %);

(c) 20 metric tons of depleted uranium with an *enrichment* of 0.005 (0.5 %) or below; and

(d) 20 metric tons of thorium.

25. Safeguards with respect to *nuclear material* in irradiated fuel which is

transferred for the purpose of reprocessing may also be suspended if the State or States concerned have, with the agreement of the Agency, placed under safeguards substitute *nuclear material* in accordance with paragraph 26(d) for the period of suspension. In addition. safeguards with respect to plutonium contained in irradiated fuel which is transferred for the purpose of reprocessing may be suspended for a period not to exceed six months if the State or States concerned have, with the agreement of the Agency, placed under safeguards a quantity of uranium whose *enrichment* in the isotope uranium-235 is not less than 0.9 (90 %) and the uranium-235 content of which is equal in weight to such plutonium. Upon expiration of the said six months or the completion of reprocessing, whichever is earlier, safeguards shall, with the agreement of the Agency, be applied to such plutonium and shall cease to apply to the uranium substituted therefor.

D. Termination of safeguards

26. *Nuclear material* shall no longer be subject to safeguards after:

(*a*) It has been returned to the State that originally supplied it (whether directly or through the Agency), if it was subject to safeguards only by reason of such supply and if:

   (i) It was not *improved* while under safeguards; or
   (ii) Any special fissionable material that was produced in it under safeguards has been separated out, or safeguards with respect to such produced material have been terminated; or

(*b*) The Agency has determined that:

   (i) It was subject to safeguards only by reason of its use in a *principal nuclear facility* specified in paragraph 19(d);
   (ii) It has been removed from such facility; and
   (iii) Any special fissionable material that was produced in it under safeguards has been separated out, or safeguards with respect to such produced material have been terminated; or

(*c*) The Agency has determined that it has been consumed, or has been diluted in such a way that it is no longer usable for any nuclear activity relevant from the point of view of safeguards, or has become practicably irrecoverable; or

(*d*) The State or States concerned have, with the agreement of the Agency, placed under safeguards, as a substitute, such amount of the same element, not otherwise subject to safeguards, as the Agency has determined contains fissionable isotopes:

   (i) Whose weight (with due allowance for processing losses) is equal to or greater than the weight of the fissionable isotopes of the material with respect to which safeguards are to terminate; and
   (ii) Whose ratio by weight to the total substituted element is similar to or greater than the ratio by weight of the fissionable isotopes of the material with respect to which safeguards are to terminate to the total wight of such material;

provided that the Agency may agree to the substitution of plutonium for uranium-235 contained in uranium whose *enrichment* is not greater than 0.05 (5.0%); or

(*e*) It has been transferred out of the State under paragraph 28(d), provided that such material shall again be subject to safeguards if it is returned to the State in which the Agency had safeguarded it; or

(*f*) The conditions specified in the *safeguards agreement*, pursuant to which it was subject to Agency safeguards, no longer apply, by expiration of the agreement or otherwise.

27. If a State wishes to use safeguarded source material for non-nuclear purposes, such as the production of alloys or ceramics, it shall agree with the Agency on the circumstances under which the safeguards on such material may be terminated.

E. Transfer of safeguarded nuclear material out of the state

28. No safeguarded *nuclear material* shall be transferred outside the jurisdiction of the State in which it is being safeguarded until the Agency has satisfied itself that one or more of the following conditions apply:

(a) The material is being returned, under the conditions specified in paragraph 26(a), to the State that originally supplied it; or

(b) The material is being transferred subject to the provisions of paragraph 24 or 25; or

(c) Arrangements have been made by the Agency to safeguard the material in accordance with this document in the State to which it is being transferred; or

(d) The material was not subject to safeguards pursuant to a *project agreement* and will be subject, in the State to which it is being transferred, to safeguards other than those of the Agency but generally consistent with such safeguards and accepted by the Agency.

III. *Safeguards procedures*

A. General procedures

Introduction

29. The safeguards procedures set forth below shall be followed, as far as relevant, with respect to safeguarded *nuclear materials*, whether they are being produced, processed or used in any *principal nuclear facility* or are outside any such facility. These procedures also extend to facilities containing or to contain such materials, including *principal nuclear facilities* to which the criteria in paragraph 19(d) apply.

Design review

30. The Agency shall review the design of *principal nuclear facilities*, for the sole purpose of satisfying itself that a facility will permit the effective application of safeguards.

31. The design review of a *principal nuclear facility* shall take place at as early a stage as possible. In particular, such review shall be carried out in the case of:

(a) An Agency project, before the project is approved;

(b) A bilateral or multilateral arrangement under which the responsibility for administering safeguards is to be transferred to the Agency, or an activity *unilaterally submitted* by a State, before the Agency assumes safeguards responsibilities with respect to the facility;

(c) A transfer of safeguarded *nuclear material* to a *principal nuclear facility* whose design has not previously been reviewed, before such transfer takes place; and

(d) A significant modification of a *principal nuclear facility* whose design has previously been reviewed, before such modification is undertaken.

32. To enable the Agency to perform the required design review, the State shall submit to it relevant design information sufficient for the purpose, including

information on such basic characteristics of the *principal nuclear facility* as may bear on the Agency's safeguards procedures. The Agency shall require only the minimum amount of information and data consistent with carrying out its responsibility under this section. It shall complete the review promptly after the submission of this information by the State and shall notify the latter of its conclusions without delay.

Records

33. The State shall arrange for the keeping of records with respect to *principal nuclear facilities* and also with respect to all safeguarded *nuclear material* outside such facilities. For this purpose the State and the Agency shall agree on a system of records with respect to each facility and also with respect to such material, on the basis of proposals to be submitted by the State in sufficient time to allow the Agency to review them before the records need to be kept.

34. If the records are not kept in one of the working languages of the Board, the State shall make arrangements to facilitate their examination by inspectors.

35. The records shall consist, as appropriate, of:

(*a*) Accounting records of all safeguarded *nuclear material*; and

(*b*) Operating records for *principal nuclear facilities*.

36. All records shall be retained for at least two years.

Reports

GENERAL REQUIREMENTS

37. The State shall submit to the Agency reports with respect to the production, processing and use of safeguarded *nuclear material* in or outside *principal nuclear facilities*. For this purpose the State and the Agency shall agree on a system of reports with respect to each facility and also with respect to safeguarded *nuclear material* outside such facilities, on the basis of proposals to be submitted by the State in sufficient time to allow the Agency to review them before the reports need to be submitted. The reports need include only such information as is relevant for the purpose of safeguards.

38. Unless otherwise provided in the applicable *safeguards agreement*, reports shall be submitted in one of the working languages of the Board.

ROUTINE REPORTS

39. Routine reports shall be based on the records compiled in accordance with paragraphs 33–36 and shall consist, as appropriate, of:

(*a*) Accounting reports showing the receipt, transfer out, inventory and use of all safeguarded *nuclear material*. The inventory shall indicate the nuclear and chemical composition and physical form of all material and its location on the date of the report; and

(*b*) Operating reports showing the use that has been made of each *principal nuclear facility* since the last report and, as far as possible, the programme of future work in the period until the next routine report is expected to reach the Agency.

40. The first routine report shall be submitted as soon as:

(*a*) There is any safeguarded *nuclear material* to be accounted for; or

(*b*) The *principal nuclear facility* to which it relates is in a condition to operate.

PROGRESS IN CONSTRUCTION

41. The Agency may, if so provided in a *safeguards agreement*, request information as to when particular stages in the construction of a *principal nuclear facility* have been or are to be reached.

SPECIAL REPORTS

42. The State shall report to the Agency without delay:

(*a*) If any unusual incident occurs involving actual or potential loss or destruction of, or damage to, any safeguarded *nuclear material* or *principal nuclear facility*; or

(*b*) If there is good reason to believe that safeguarded *nuclear material* is lost or unaccounted for in quantities that exceed the normal operating and handling losses that have been accepted by the Agency as characteristic of the facility.

43. The State shall report to the Agency, as soon as possible, and in any case within two weeks, any transfer not requiring advance notification that will result in a significant change (to be defined by the Agency in agreement with the State) in the quantity of safeguarded *nuclear material* in a facility, or in a complex of facilities considered as a unit for this purpose by agreement with the Agency. Such report shall indicate the amount and nature of the material and its intended use.

AMPLIFICATION OF REPORTS

44. At the Agency's request the State shall submit amplifications or clarifications of any report, in so far as relevant for the purpose of safeguards.

Inspections

GENERAL PROCEDURES

45. The Agency may inspect safeguarded *nuclear materials* and *principal nuclear facilities*.

46. The purpose of safeguards inspections shall be to verify compliance with *safeguards agreements* and to assist States in complying with such agreements and in resolving any questions arising out of the implementation of safeguards.

47. The number, duration and intensity of inspections actually carried out shall be kept to the minimum consistent with the effective implementation of safeguards, and if the Agency considers that the authorized inspections are not all required, fewer shall be carried out.

48. Inspectors shall neither operate any facility themselves nor direct the staff of a facility to carry out any particular operation.

ROUTINE INSPECTIONS

49. Routine inspections may include, as appropriate:

(*a*) Audit of records and reports;

(*b*) Verification of the amount of safeguarded *nuclear material* by physical inspection, measurement and sampling;

(*c*) Examination of *principal nuclear facilities*, including a check of their measuring instruments and operating characteristics; and

(*d*) Check of the operations carried out at *principal nuclear facilities* and at *research and development facilities* containing safeguarded *nuclear material*.

50. Whenever the Agency has the right of access to a *principal nuclear facility* at

all times[2] it may perform inspections of which notice as required by paragraph 4 of the *Inspectors Document* need not be given, in so far as this is necessary for the effective application of safeguards. The actual procedures to implement these provisions shall be agreed upon between the parties concerned in the *safeguards agreement*.

INITIAL INSPECTIONS OF PRINCIPAL NUCLEAR FACILITIES

51. To verify that the construction of a *principal nuclear facility* is in accordance with the design reviewed by the Agency, an initial inspection or inspections of the facility may be carried out, if so provided in a *safeguards agreement*:

(*a*) As soon as possible after the facility has come under Agency safeguards, in the case of a facility already in operation; or

(*b*) Before the facility starts to operate, in other cases.

52. The measuring instruments and operating characteristics of the facility shall be reviewed to the extent necessary for the purpose of implementing safeguards. Instruments that will be used to obtain data on the *nuclear materials* in the facility may be tested to determine their satisfactory functioning. Such testing may include the observation by inspectors of commissioning or routine tests by the staff of the facility, but shall not hamper or delay the construction, commissioning or normal operation of the facility.

SPECIAL INSPECTIONS

53. The Agency may carry out special inspections if:

(*a*) The study of a report indicates that such inspection is desirable; or

(*b*) Any unforeseen circumstance requires immediate action.

The Board shall subsequently be informed of the reasons for and the results of each such inspection.

54. The Agency may also carry out special inspections of substantial amounts of safeguarded *nuclear material* that are to be transferred outside the jurisdiction of the State in which it is being safeguarded, for which purpose the State shall give the Agency sufficient advance notice of any such proposed transfer.

B. Special procedures for reactors

Reports

55. The frequency of submission of routine reports shall be agreed between the Agency and the State, taking into account the frequency established for routine inspections. However, at least two such reports shall be submitted each year and in no case shall more than 12 such reports be required in any year.

Inspections

56. One of the initial inspections of a *reactor* shall if possible be made just before the reactor first reaches criticality.

57. The maximum frequency of routine inspections of a *reactor* and of the safeguarded *nuclear material* in it shall be determined from the following table:

[2] See paragraph 57.

Whichever is the largest of: (a) Facility inventory (including loading); (b) Annual throughput; (c) Maximum potential annual production of special fissionable material (*Effective kilograms of nuclear material*)	Maximum number of routine inspections annually
Up to 1	0
More than 1 and up to 5	1
More than 5 and up to 10	2
More than 10 and up to 15	3
More than 15 and up to 20	4
More than 20 and up to 25	5
More than 25 and up to 30	6
More than 30 and up to 35	7
More than 35 and up to 40	8
More than 40 and up to 45	9
More than 45 and up to 50	10
More than 50 and up to 55	11
More than 55 and up to 60	12
More than 60	Right of access at all times

58. The actual frequency of inspection of a *reactor* shall take account of:

(*a*) Whether the State possesses irradiated-fuel reprocessing facilities;

(*b*) The nature of the *reactor*; and

(*c*) The nature and amount of the *nuclear material* produced or used in the *reactor*.

C. Special procedures relating to safeguarded nuclear material outside principal nuclear facilities

Nuclear material in research and development facilities

ROUTINE REPORTS

59. Only accounting reports need be submitted in respect of *nuclear material* in *research and development facilities*. The frequency of submission of such routine reports shall be agreed between the Agency and the State, taking into account the frequency established for routine inspections; however, at least one such report shall be submitted each year and in no case shall more than 12 such reports be required in any year.

ROUTINE INSPECTIONS

60. The maximum frequency of routine inspections of safeguarded *nuclear material* in a *research and development facility* shall be that specified in the table in paragraph 57 for the total amount of material in the facility.

Source material in sealed storage

61. The following simplified procedures for safeguarding stockpiled source material shall be applied if a State undertakes to store such material in a sealed storage facility and not to remove it therefrom without previously informing the Agency.

DESIGN OF STORAGE FACILITIES

62. The State shall submit to the Agency information on the design of each sealed storage facility and agree with the Agency on the method and procedure for sealing it.

ROUTINE REPORTS

63. Two routine accounting reports in respect of source material in sealed storage shall be submitted each year.

ROUTINE INSPECTIONS

64. The Agency may perform one routine inspection of each sealed storage facility annually.

REMOVAL OF MATERIAL

65. The State may remove safeguarded source material from a sealed storage facility after informing the Agency of the amount, type and intended use of the material to be removed, and providing sufficient other data in time to enable the Agency to continue safeguarding the material after it has been removed.

Nuclear material in other locations

66. Except to the extent that safeguarded *nuclear material* outside of *principal nuclear facilities* is covered by any of the provisions set forth in paragraphs 59–65, the following procedures shall be applied with respect to such material (for example, source material stored elsewhere than in a sealed storage facility, or special fissionable material used in a sealed neutron source in the field).

ROUTINE REPORTS

67. Routine accounting reports in respect of all safeguarded *nuclear material* in this category shall be submitted periodically. The frequency of submission of such reports shall be agreed between the Agency and the State, taking into account the frequency established for routine inspections; however, at least one such report shall be submitted each year and in no case shall more than 12 such reports be required in any year.

ROUTINE INSPECTIONS

68. The maximum frequency of routine inspections of safeguarded *nuclear material* in this category shall be one inspection annually if the total amount of such material does not exceed five *effective kilograms*, and shall be determined from the table in paragraph 57 if the amount is greater.

IV. *Definitions*

69. "Agency" means the International Atomic Energy Agency.

70. "Board" means the Board of Governors of the Agency.

71. "Director General" means the Director General of the Agency.

72. "Effective kilograms" means:

(a) In the case of plutonium, its weight in kilograms;

(b) In the case of uranium with an *enrichment* of 0.01 (1 %) and above, its weight in kilograms multiplied by the square of its *enrichment*;

(c) In the case of uranium with an *enrichment* below 0.01 (1 %) and above 0.005 (0.5 %), its weight in kilograms multiplied by 0.0001; and

(d) In the case of depleted uranium with an *enrichment* of 0.005 (0.5 %) or below, and in the case of thorium, its weight in kilograms multiplied by 0.00005.

73. "Enrichment" means the ratio of the combined weight of the isotopes uranium-233 and uranium-235 to that of the total uranium in question.

74. "Improved" means, with respect to *nuclear material* that either:

(a) The concentration of fissionable isotopes in it has been increased; or

(b) The amount of chemically separable fissionable isotopes in it has been increased; or

(c) Its chemical or physical form has been changed so as to facilitate further use or processing.

75. "Inspector" means an Agency official designated in accordance with the *Inspectors Document*.

76. "Inspectors Document" means the Annex to the Agency's document GC(V)/INF/39.

77. "Nuclear material" means any source or special fissionable material as defined in Article XX of the Statute.

78. "Principal nuclear facility" means a *reactor*, a plant for processing *nuclear material* irradiated in a *reactor*, a plant for separating the isotopes of a *nuclear material*, a plant for processing or fabricating *nuclear material* (excepting a mine or ore-processing plant) or a facility or plant of such other type as may be designated by the Board from time to time, including associated storage facilities.

79. "Project agreement" means a *safeguards agreement* relating to an Agency project and containing provisions as foreseen in Article XI.F.4(b) of the Statute.

80. "Reactor" means any device in which a controlled, self-sustaining fission chain-reaction can be maintained.

81. "Research and development facility" means a facility, other than a *principal nuclear facility*, used for research or development in the field of nuclear energy.

82. "Safeguards agreement" means an agreement between the Agency and one or more Member States which contains an undertaking by one or more of those States not to use certain items in such a way as to further any military purpose and which gives the Agency the right to observe compliance with such undertaking. Such an agreement may concern:

(a) An Agency project;

(b) A bilateral or multilateral arrangement in the field of nuclear energy under which the Agency may be asked to administer safeguards; or

(c) Any of a State's nuclear activities *unilaterally submitted* to Agency safeguards.

83. "Statute" means the Statute of the Agency.

84. "Throughput" means the rate at which *nuclear material* is introduced into a facility operating at full capacity.

85. "Unilaterally submitted" means submitted by a State to Agency safeguards, pursuant to a *safeguards agreement*.

Annex II. Provisions for reprocessing plants

Introduction

1. The Agency's Safeguards System (1965) is so formulated as to permit application to *principal nuclear facilities* other than *reactors* as foreseen in paragraph 7. This Annex lays down the additional procedures which are applicable to the safeguarding of *reprocessing plants*. However, because of the possible need to revise these procedures in the light of experience, they shall be subject to review at any time and shall in any case be reviewed after two years' experience of their application has been gained.

Special procedures

Reports

2. The frequency of submission of routine reports shall be once each calendar month.

Inspections

3. A *reprocessing plant* having an annual *throughput* not exceeding 5 *effective kilograms* of *nuclear material*, and the safeguarded *nuclear material* in it, may be routinely inspected twice a year. A *reprocessing plant* having an annual *throughput* exceeding 5 *effective kilograms* of *nuclear material* and the safeguarded *nuclear material* in it, may be inspected at all times. The arrangements for inspections set forth in paragraph 50 shall apply to all inspections to be made under this paragraph.[1]

4. When a *reprocessing plant* is under Agency safeguards only because it contains safeguarded *nuclear material*, the inspection frequency shall be based on the rate of delivery of safeguarded *nuclear material*.

5. The State and the Agency shall co-operate in making all the necessary arrangements to facilitate the taking, shipping or analysis of samples, due account being taken of the limitations imposed by the characteristics of a plant already in operation when placed under Agency safeguards.

Mixtures of safeguarded and unsafeguarded nuclear material

6. By agreement between the State and the Agency, the following special arrangements may be made in the case of a *reprocessing plant* to which the criteria in paragraph 19(d) do not apply, and in which safeguarded and unsafeguarded *nuclear materials* are present:

(a) Subject to the provisions of sub-paragraph (b) below, the Agency shall restrict its safeguards procedures to the area in which irradiated fuel is stored, until such time as all or any part of such fuel is transferred out of the storage area into other parts of the plant. Safeguards procedures shall cease to apply to the storage area or plant when either contains no safeguarded *nuclear material*; and

(b) Where possible safeguarded *nuclear material* shall be measured and sampled separately from unsafeguarded material, and at as early a stage as possible. Where separate measurement, sampling or processing are not possible, the whole of the material being processed in that *campaign* shall be subject to the

---

[1] It is understood that for plants having an annual *throughput* of more than 60 *effective kilograms*, the right of access at all times would normally be implemented by means of continuous inspection.

safeguards procedures set out in this Annex. At the conclusion of the processing the *nuclear material* that is thereafter to be safeguarded shall be selected by agreement between the State and the Agency from the whole output of the plant resulting from that *campaign*, due account being taken of any processing losses accepted by the Agency.

Definitions

7. "Reprocessing plant"[2] means a facility to separate irradiated *nuclear materials* and fission products, and includes the facility's head-end treatment section and its associated storage and analytical sections.

8. "Campaign" means the period during which the chemical processing equipment in a *reprocessing plant* is operated between two successive wash-outs of the *nuclear material* present in the equipment.

[2] This term is synonymous with the term "a plant for processing nuclear material irradiated in a reactor" which is used in paragraph 78.

Annex II. Provisions for safeguarded nuclear material in conversion plants and fabrication plants

Introduction

1. The Agency's Safeguards System (1965, as Provisionally Extended in 1966) is so formulated as to permit application to *principal nuclear facilities* other than *reactors* as foreseen in paragraph 7. This Annex lays down the additional procedures which are applicable to safeguarded *nuclear material* in *conversion plants* and *fabrication plants*[1]. However, because of the possible need to revise these procedures in the light of experience, they shall be subject to review at any time and shall in any case be reviewed after two years' experience of their application has been gained.

Special procedures

Reports

2. The frequency of submission of routine reports shall be once each calendar month.

Inspections

3. A *conversion plant* or *fabrication plant* to which the criteria in paragraph 19(d) apply and the *nuclear material* in it, may be inspected at all times if the plant inventory at any time, or the annual input, of *nuclear material* exceeds five *effective kilograms*. Where neither the inventory at any time, nor the annual input, exceeds five *effective kilograms* of *nuclear material*, the routine inspections shall not exceed two a year. The arrangements for inspection set forth in paragraph 50 shall apply to all inspections to be made under this paragraph[2].

4. When a *conversion plant* or *fabrication plant* to which the criteria in paragraph 19(d) do not apply contains safeguarded *nuclear material* the frequency of routine inspections shall be based on the inventory at any time and the annual input of safeguarded *nuclear material*. Where the inventory at any time, or the annual input, of safeguarded *nuclear material* exceeds five *effective kilograms* the plant may be inspected at all times. Where neither the inventory at any time, nor the annual input, exceeds five *effective kilograms* of safeguarded *nuclear material* the routine inspections shall not exceed two a year. The arrangements for inspection set forth in paragraph 50 shall apply to all inspections to be made under this paragraph[2].

5. The intensity of inspection of safeguarded *nuclear material* at various steps in a *conversion plant* or *fabrication plant* shall take account of the nature, isotopic composition and amount of safeguarded *nuclear material* in the plant. Safeguards shall be applied in accordance with the general principles set forth in paragraphs 9–14. Emphasis shall be placed on inspection to control uranium of high enrichments and plutonium.

---

[1] This terminology is intended to be synonymous with the term "a plant for processing or fabricating *nuclear material* (excepting a mine or ore-processing plant") which is used in paragraph 78.

[2] It is understood that for plants having an inventory at any time, or an annual input, of more than *60 effective kilograms* the right of access at all times would normally be implemented by means of continuous inspection. Where neither the inventory at any time nor the annual input exceeds one *effective kilogram* of *nuclear material* the plant would not normally be subject to routine inspection.

6. Where a plant may handle safeguarded and unsafeguarded *nuclear material,* the State shall notify the Agency in advance of the programme for handling safeguarded batches to enable the Agency to make inspections during these periods, due account being also taken of the arrangements under paragraph 10 below.

7. The State and the Agency shall co-operate in making all the necessary arrangements to facilitate the preparation of inventories of safeguarded *nuclear material* and the taking, shipping and/or analysis of samples, due account being taken of the limitations imposed by the characteristics of a plant already in operation when placed under Agency safeguards.

Residues, scrap and waste

8. The State shall ensure that safeguarded *nuclear material* contained in residues, scrap or waste created during conversion or fabrication is recovered, as far as is practicable, in its facilities and within a reasonable period of time. If such recovery is not considered practicable by the State, the State and the Agency shall co-operate in making arrangements to account for and dispose of the material.

Safeguarded and unsafeguarded nuclear material

9. By agreement between the State and the Agency, the following arrangements may be made in the case of a *conversion plant* or a *fabrication plant* to which the criteria in paragraph 19(d) do not apply, and in which safeguarded and unsafeguarded *nuclear material* are both present:

(*a*) Subject to the provisions of sub-paragraph (*b*) below, the Agency shall restrict its safeguards procedures to the area in which safeguarded *nuclear material* is stored, until such time as all or any part of such *nuclear material* is transferred out of the storage area into other parts of the plant. Safeguards procedures shall cease to be applied to the storage area or plant when it contains no safeguarded *nuclear material;* and

(*b*) Where possible, safeguarded *nuclear material* shall be measured and sampled separately from unsafeguarded *nuclear material*, and at as early a stage as possible. Where separate measurement, sampling or processing is not possible, any *nuclear material* containing safeguarded *nuclear material* shall be subject to the safeguards procedures set out in this Annex. At the conclusion of processing, the *nuclear material* that is thereafter to be safeguarded shall be selected, in accordance with paragraph 11 below when applicable, by agreement between the State and the Agency, due account being taken of any processing losses accepted by the Agency.

Blending of nuclear material

10. When safeguarded *nuclear material* is to be blended with either safeguarded or unsafeguarded *nuclear material*, the State shall notify the Agency sufficiently in advance of the programme of blending to enable the Agency to exercise its right to obtain evidence, through inspection of the blending operation or otherwise, that the blending is performed according to the programme.

11. When safeguarded and unsafeguarded *nuclear material* are blended, if the ratio of fissionable isotopes in the safeguarded component going into the blend to all the fissionable isotopes in the blend is 0.3 or greater, and if the concentration of fissionable isotopes in the unsafeguarded *nuclear material* is increased by such blending, then the whole bland shall remain subject to safeguards. In other cases the following procedures shall apply:

(*a*) Plutonium/plutonium blending. The quantity of the blend that shall continue to be safeguarded shall be such that its weight, when multiplied by the square of the weight fraction of contained fissionable isotopes, is not less than the weight of originally safeguarded plutonium multiplied by the square of the weight fraction of fissionable isotopes therein, provided however that:

(i) In cases where the weight of the whole blend, when multiplied by the square of the weight fraction of contained fissionable isotopes, is less than the weight of originally safeguarded plutonium multiplied by the square of the weight fraction of fissionable isotopes therein, the whole of the blend shall be safeguarded; and

(ii) The number of fissionable atoms in the portion of the blend that shall continue to be under safeguards shall in no case be less than the number of fissionable atoms in the originally safeguarded plutonium;

(b) Uranium/uranium blending. The quantity of the blend that shall continue to be safeguarded shall be such that the number of *effective kilograms* is not less than the number of *effective kilograms* in the originally safeguarded uranium, provided however that:

(i) In cases where the number of *effective kilograms* in the whole blend is less than in the safeguarded uranium, the whole of the blend shall be safeguarded, and

(ii) The number of fissionable atoms in the portion of the blend that shall continue to be under safeguards shall in no case be less than the number of fissionable atoms in the originally safeguarded uranium;

(c) Uranium/plutonium blending. The whole of the resultant blend shall be safeguarded until the uranium and the plutonium constituents are separated. After separation of the uranium and plutonium, safeguards shall apply to the originally safeguarded component; and

(d) Due account shall be taken of any processing losses agreed upon between the State and the Agency.

Definitions

12. "Conversion plant" means a facility (excepting a mine or ore-processing plant) to *improve* unirradiated *nuclear material*, or irradiated *nuclear material* that has been separated from fission products, by changing its chemical or physical form so as to facilitate further use or processing. The term *conversion plant* includes the facility's storage and analytical sections. The term does not include a plant intended for separating the isotopes of a *nuclear material*.

13. "Fabrication plant" means a plant to manufacture fuel elements or other components containing *nuclear material* and includes the plant's storage and analytical sections.

Appendix 5

The Agency's inspectorate

Annex 5: Memorandum by the Director General:
[GD(V)INF/39]

I. Designation[1] of Agency inspectors

1. When it is proposed to designate an Agency inspector for a State, the Director General shall inform the State in writing of the name, nationality and grade of the Agency inspector proposed, shall transmit a written certification of his relevant qualifications and shall enter into such other consultations as the State may request. The State shall inform the Director General, within 30 days of receipt of such proposal, whether it accepts the designation of that inspector. If so, the inspector may be designated as one of the Agency's inspectors for that State, and the Director General shall notify the State concerned of such designation.

2. If a State, either upon proposal of a designation or at any time after a designation has been made, objects to the designation of an Agency inspector for that State, it shall inform the Director General of its objection. In this event, the Director General shall propose to the State an alternative designation or designations. The Director General may refer to the Board, for its appropriate action, the repeated refusal of a State to accept the designation of an Agency inspector if, in his opinion, this refusal would impede the inspections provided for in the relevant project or safeguards agreement.

3. Each State shall as speedily as possible grant or renew appropriate visas, where required, for persons whose designation as Agency inspectors that State has accepted.

II. Visits of Agency inspectors

4. The State shall be given at least one week's notice of each inspection, including the names of the Agency's inspectors, the place and approximate time of their arrival and departure, and the facilities and materials to be inspected. Such notice need not exceed 24 hours for any inspection to investigate any incident requiring a "special inspection".

5. Agency inspectors shall be accompanied by representatives of the State concerned, if the State so requests, provided that the inspectors shall not thereby be delayed or otherwise impeded in the exercise of their functions. Agency inspectors shall use such points of entry into and departure from the State, and such routes and modes of travel within it, as may be designated by the State.

6. Agency inspectors, in locations where this is necessary, shall be provided, on request and for reasonable compensation if agreed on, with appropriate equipment for carrying out inspections and with suitable accomodation and transport.

7. The visits and activities of the Agency's inspectors shall be so arranged as to ensure on the one hand the effective discharge of their functions and on the other hand the minimum possible inconvenience to the State and disturbance to the facilities inspected.

[1] The term "designation" as used in this Annex refers to the assignment of Agency inspectors to a particular task or tasks and not to the recruitment or appointment of Agency inspectors.

8. Consultations shall take place with the State to ensure that consistent with the effective discharge of the functions of the Agency's inspectors, their activities will be conducted in harmony with the laws and regulations existing in the State.

III. Rights of access and inspection

9. After submitting their credentials, and to the extent relevant to the project or arrangement, Agency inspectors shall have access, depending upon the type of inspection to be carried out, either:

(a) To all materials, equipment and facilities to which Agency safeguards against diversion are applied under the relevant provisions of document INFCIRC/26; or

(b) To all radiation sources, equipment and facilities which can be inspected by those Agency inspectors who are making inspections in relation to the provisions of paragraphs 31 and 32 of the Agency's health and safety measures set forth in document INFCIRC/18.

They shall have access at all times to all places and data and to any person, to the extent provided for in Article XII.A.6 of the Statute. The State shall direct all such persons under its control to co-operate fully with Agency inspectors, and shall indicate the exact location of and identify all such materials, equipment and facilities.

10. With respect to all materials, equipment and facilities to which Agency safeguards against diversion are applied, the Agency's inspectors shall be permitted to carry out their inspections in accordance with the pertinent agreements which may include provisions for:

(a) Examination of the facility and/or materials to which Agency safeguards are applied;

(b) Audit of reports and records;

(c) Verification of the amounts of material to which Agency safeguards are applied, by physical inspection, measurement and sampling; and

(d) Examination and testing of the measurement instruments.

11. Agency inspectors for health and safety measures may perform inspections in accordance with each individual agreement, which may necessitate:

(a) Tests of radiation sources, of radiation detection and monitoring instruments and of other equipment or devices in connection with the use, storage, transportation or disposal as waste of radiation sources.;

(b) Examination of facilities wherein radiation sources are used or stored, of waste disposal facilities and of all records on which reports to the Agency are based; and

(c) Examinations related to the evaluation of the radiation exposure of persons who have or may have been over-exposed.

The State shall perform, in a manner prescribed by the Agency, or arrange for the Agency to perform those tests and examinations deemed necessary by the Agency.

12. After an inspection has been carried out, the State, concerned shall be duly informed by the Agency of its results. In case the State disagrees with the report of the Agency's inspectors, it shall be entitled to submit a report on the matter to the Board of Governors.

IV. The privileges and immunities of the Agency's inspectors

13. Agency inspectors shall be granted the privileges and immunities necessary for the performance of their functions. Suitable provision shall be included in each project or safeguards agreement for the application, in so far as relevant to the execution of that agreement, of the provisions of the Agreement on the Privileges and Immunities of the International Atomic Energy Agency excepting Articles V and XII thereof, provided that all parties to the project or safeguards agreement so agree.

14. Disputes between a State and the Agency arising out of the exercise of the functions of Agency inspectors will be settled according to an appropriate disputes clause in the pertinent project or safeguards agreement.

DATE DUE

MAR 1 4 1979			
NOV 1 9 1980			
APR 2 8 1982			
MAY 3 1 1997			
GAYLORD			PRINTED IN U.S.A.